W9-CHG-486

Roses

ROSES

OLD ROSES AND SPECIES ROSES

Photographs PAUL STAROSTA
Text ELÉONORE CRUSE

The rose, queen of flowers

The wild rose grows in fields, on banks, and beside ditches, where nature runs wild and children like to pick the little red fruits in early winter. At first glance, wild roses all look much the same. As for cultivated roses, they are grown everywhere: on railway stations, in kitchen gardens among the vegetables, in every tiny town garden, in cemeteries... They clamber up walls, they are trained on trellises, they adorn our parks. They might even be considered invasive, so insistently do they make their way into our daily lives. We have been spellbound by the rose since very early times. It is still surprising to find the loveliest, sweetest, and most fragrant flowers of all blooming on stems armed with such sharp thorns, yet those thorns do not deter the real rose-lover. Whether in the form of naturally occurring wild or species roses (sometimes called botanical roses), or as the cultivated roses grown in our gardens, the rose is generally considered the queen of flowers. And as the very word "queen" suggests, it has a long history.

The rose belongs to the Rosaceae family, along with other domesticated plants such as the apple, pear, cherry, plum, and strawberry, as well as a number of ornamental plants. However, it is the only member of the genus Rosa, defined as a woody, deciduous shrub, with thorny or occasionally smooth stems, leaves made up of leaflets,* and flowers which usually have five petals.

Originally roses grew only in the wild, and were subject to genetic change brought about by unknown factors. Subsequent human intervention has changed their shape and appearance in many different ways, and the outcome has been the introduction of a large number of varieties* as they are known today.

The term "old roses" is generally agreed to apply to all roses bred before 1920. However, this book will also deal with a few which, although introduced later, are the direct descendants of old roses and are not usually classed with modern roses.

Collectors gather as much information as possible to help with the dating, identification and preservation of the oldest roses of all. Certain characteristics, although they may not be very strongly marked, enable us to distinguish between old roses and roses bred by modern horticulturalists. Modern roses have large, shiny leaves consisting of five leaflets, arranged at regular intervals along the branches of the bush; the appearance of the leaves does not change much from one variety to another, while old roses have more variety in their leaves, which are made up of smaller, more numerous leaflets. The stems of modern roses, bearing strong thorns, are straighter and stiffer than those of old roses, which are often flexible and inclined to droop, and are covered with many small thorns.

Old roses therefore have a less rigid habit of growth and denser foliage, giving them the look of wild plants, further accentuated by the fact that they are not pruned hard. When we come to the Hybrid Teas and Hybrid Perpetuals, however, it is more difficult to draw a distinction between old and modern roses.

Trying to date a variety and identify it precisely is a fascinating exercise, and may take several years of research. It is rather like the expert identification of old pictures. Archive materials can provide evidence to support the conclusions of researchers, and since the nineteenth century so can botanic gardens. With their aid, we can go back in time.

Above

Rosier Floribunda 'Gruss an Aachen' (× 0.85)

The classification of old roses

Botanic gardens label their plants, and are good places to learn more about the different categories of roses:

Wild roses

These large shrubs are members of the Rosaceae family, and grow naturally in the wild. Labels in botanic gardens will usually mention their place of geographical origin. It is interesting to see that although some wild species can be found from the Arctic Circle (*Rosa acicularis*) to the south of Abyssinia, there is none indigenous to the southern hemisphere. The same is true of several hundred wild roses (or eglantines) and identified species roses.

Like all plants, a rose has a scientific Latin name. Sometimes it incorporates the name of the person who discovered or introduced that particular rose, Latinized and made part of the species name. For instance, *Rosa hugonis* means "Father Hugo's rose", from the name of the missionary who discovered it in China in 1899. Species roses are the ancestors of old varieties and are closely linked to them, thus defining the section* to which those varieties belong. Some roses are the offspring of a species which is itself the product of a cross between two species, i.e. it is a hybrid species. In that case the label will say, for instance, *Rosa* × *alba* 'Celestial', meaning that the variety 'Celestial' is descended from the *Rosa* × *alba* group, which is a hybrid itself, hence the ×.

The earliest varieties: an enigma

Some roses are identified by a variety name without any indication of the date of introduction* or the breeder.* The only information given may be the name of the section to which they belong. These are among the oldest of roses, part of our plant heritage. We do not know their origins precisely, and we could not re-create them if they died out, so it is important to ensure their survival by propagation.

Besides the charmingly old-fashioned or literary nature of some of the names of these rose varieties, we can tell that they are very old by analyzing the characteristics of their section. Points to observe are the texture, shape, colour, and density of the foliage, the structure of the buds and flowers, the appearance of the stems and thorns, and the whole plant's habit of growth.

Roses are mentioned by name in a number of old books. Comparing different descriptions in order to identify a plant is an absorbing process, but obviously there may be errors: living plants are unlikely to be preserved from generation to generation absolutely unchanged. Methodical labelling did not begin until the nineteenth century, practised by a handful of enthusiasts. Mentions in Greek and Latin literature (Herodotus, Theophrastus, Pliny the Elder) are all we have to help us recognize the very oldest of roses. There are also some depictions of roses on frescos, for instance at Knossos on Crete, but they are not sufficiently detailed for purposes of identification.

Another mystery surrounds certain roses such as 'Belle de Crécy'. Are they the product of human intervention, by hybridization or seed selection? Did the wind or insect pollination get in first and do the breeder's work for him, or did natural mutations occur as a result of improvements in growing conditions? These questions lead to others: how long has horticulture itself been practised? Where did it begin? The answer is probably in Asia Minor, in the heart of ancient Persia – on the terraces of the Hanging Gardens of Babylon.

Identified varieties

We have enough information about these roses to date their breeding, name their breeders, and give the names of their parents (unless the breeders did not disclose them), so that we know of which varieties they have retained the characteristics, properties, and even perfume. These roses have historical records behind them, and are mentioned in a number of documents or nurserymen's catalogues from the nineteenth century onwards.

It is quite common for the name of a variety to be followed by one or more synonyms. Preferred names may vary from country to country, and it is usual to mention them all, because they are elements in determining the identity of the rose. For instance, 'Cuisse de Nymphe' (the most usual name for this rose in France) is also known as 'Maiden's Blush' (the most usual name in England), 'La Virginale', 'La Royale', 'La Séduisante', 'Rosier Blanc Royal', *Rosa carnea*, and *Rosa rubicans*.

The different sections of species and their hybrids

Several hundred wild species have been recorded, although so far there is no official inventory. Most have single flowers and decorative fruits. They never suffer from disease, and look attractive all the year round. Roses are classified into sections, subdivisions of the genus *Rosa* into which species* and their hybrids* (often with double flowers) are grouped because they show similar characteristics and are obviously related.

The Caninae

The most common species in this section include *Rosa canina*, the dog rose; *Rosa rubiginosa* or sweet briar, whose crumpled foliage has a scent of green apples; *Rosa rubrifolia*, with purplish leaves, native to the mountains of Europe; and *Rosa pomifera*, which grows in the mountains of Asia. These roses are all very hardy. A hybrid species of mysterious origin, *Rosa × alba*, also belongs in this section; its pale flowers look very beautiful set off by its grey-green foliage.

The Pimpinellifoliae (or burnet roses)

The roses in this section are widely dispersed throughout Europe and Asia. Their characteristic foliage consists of small, rounded, finely dentate leaflets, resembling the leaves of burnet. They include *Rosa pimpinellifolia*, with many short, thin stems, and *Rosa foetida, Rosa hugonis*, and *Rosa xanthina*, all three yellow-flowered. Also included in this section are *Rosa farreri*, and *Rosa omeiensis*, which has flowers with four petals instead of five, and thorns that are bright red and translucent when young.

The Carolinae

The Carolinae section consists of roses originating in the east of North America: *Rosa palustris* (the 'Swamp Rose'), *Rosa virginiana, Rosa carolina, Rosa foliolosa*, and *Rosa nitida*. They sucker* very freely, and the leaves have magnificent autumn colouring. Their flowers are single and deep pink in colour.

The Cinnamomeae

There are many species in this section: *Rosa rugosa*, with its characteristic crinkled leaves, originally native to China, Japan, and Korea; *Rosa blanda*, the 'Labrador Rose'; *Rosa pendulina*, abundant in the Alps, where it does not sucker much, and in the Pyrenees where, on the contrary, it is very free-suckering on a level with the rocks; *Rosa setipoda*, which has almost no thorns and leaves with a wonderful incense scent; *Rosa moyesii*, with scarlet flowers followed by long, bottle-shaped fruits; *Rosa fedtschenkoana* from Turkestan which, unusually for a wild rose, flowers from spring until the first frosts; *Rosa multibracteata*, a magnificent shrub with flowers accompanied by many bracts;* *Rosa willmottiae*, very decorative in its habit of growth, its considerable height, and the colours of its foliage.

Above

Rosa rubrifolia (× 1.40)

The Gallicanae

This section contains a great many old varieties that have become classics. Besides *Rosa gallica* itself, there are hybrid species: *Rosa* × *centifolia*; *Rosa* × *centifolia muscosa*, the famous moss rose, romantic in appearance, with a resinous scent; *Rosa* × *damascena* and *Rosa* × *portlandica*. The Gallicanae form the basis of the horticultural genetic stock that has produced so many glorious cultivated roses. They are extremely double, with over forty petals, and none of them is yellow. Some, like 'Jacques Cartier' and 'Assemblage des Beautés', have petals incurved towards the centre; huddling beneath them are the stamens,* while the apple-green styles* form a contrast with the pink or purplish-red of the petals. The *Rosa gallica* varieties are all strongly scented. *Rosa* × *centifolia*, the cabbage rose, can bend under the weight of its deeply cupped, globular flowers. Dutch painters of the seventeenth and eighteenth centuries liked to mingle cabbage roses with fruits in their still-life pictures, in a neat allusion to the sweetness of both fruits and flowers.

The Synstylae

A characteristic of the Synstylae, a term meaning "with fused styles", is their large quantity of foliage. *Rosa multiflora, Rosa helenae, Rosa brunonii, Rosa wichuraiana, Rosa luciae, Rosa sempervirens* ("evergreen") and *Rosa arvensis* all belong to this section. They are among the most vigorous of climbing roses. The small flowers of *Rosa multiflora* are borne in large bunches or clusters and have a fresh scent. 'Veilchenblau', with a lily-of-the-valley fragrance, is particularly pretty with its mauve shades. The hybrids of *Rosa luciae* scent the air so strongly that they announce their presence the moment you enter a garden, and 'Albertine' is famous for the beauty of its flowers. None of these roses is repeat-flowering, so there is nothing to curb their vigorous climbing habit, and they become increasingly spectacular with every year that passes.

On the other hand, the Hybrid Musks, a group discovered at the beginning of the twentieth century by a clergyman, Joseph Pemberton, and developed by him and his gardeners, are extremely remontant.* These roses are descended from *Rosa multiflora, Rosa* × *noisettiana* and *Rosa chinensis*. However, *Rosa moschata*, from which the group derives the word "musk" in its name, goes very far back in time. Given deep, rich soil, the Hybrid Musks are all one could wish for in a rose.

This section also contains a group which appeared at the end of the nineteenth century: the Polyantha Roses, and their hybrids the Floribundas. Contemporary tastes in gardening called for a larger number of flowers and more repeat flowerings, and they answered these requirements. The Polyanthas were the result of crossing *Rosa multiflora* and *Rosa chinensis*, and are low-growing bushes with flowers borne in clusters, and repeat flowerings all through the summer. One of the very first Polyanthas, 'Mignonette', was bred by Guillot Fils in 1880 and was followed by many hybrids, including the still widely grown 'The Fairy'. When crossed with Hybrid Teas in the twentieth century, they produced Floribunda Roses (now often called Cluster-flowered Roses), with larger flowers borne on shrubs of the same type as the Polyanthas, making them very suitable for large, colourful displays in the flower-beds of modern parks.

The Chinenses

Also known as the Indicae, this section has given our gardens some wonderful roses. Their silky, tea-scented petals are in a wide range of soft colours, from pale yellow to coppery pink. The young leaves are reddish and smooth. A great many of them will flower almost continuously through the summer.

Early in the nineteenth century, botanists travelled to China and brought back the first specimens: *Rosa* × *odorata* and then *Rosa* × *odorata ochroleuca* and *Rosa gigantea*, which were used in the creation of the Tea Roses. They have long, supple stems. Naturally occurring varieties and a great many cultivated varieties all come under the heading of *Rosa chinensis*.

Breeders were particularly inspired by the repeat-flowering qualities of many shrubs in this section. 'Parson's Pink China', or 'Old Blush', was discovered in China at the end of the eighteenth century, brought back to England, and sent on to France and North America. It is still one of the most widely grown of the roses from the East to have survived in European climates. *Rosa moschata*, of whose mysterious origin much has been written, was crossed with 'Old Blush' in the United States, and the result was a floriferous* and charming group called *Rosa* × *noisettiana*. Using the first climbing China Roses and *Rosa* × *noisettiana*, breeders created climbing remontant roses: the Noisette Teas. In tones of yellow and pink, like 'Rêve d'Or', they have almost all the virtues one could desire. They are slightly frost-tender, so they need to be planted in a sheltered position. This section also includes Bourbon Roses, which originated in the hedges of the Ile de la Réunion, then called the Ile de Bourbon, from a cross between 'Old Blush' and 'Rose des Quatre Saisons'. They were discovered there in 1817, and then sent to France. The flowers are double or very double, cup-shaped, remontant, strongly scented, with smooth, rather sparse foliage; and few thorns, or even none at all in the case of 'Zéphirine Drouhin' and 'Kathleen Harrop'.

The Hybrid Perpetual group also comes into the Chinenses section. These roses were raised between 1830 and 1900; they are shrubs with large double flowers and, as their name indicates, either remontant or continuous-flowering. They are red or pink, more rarely white, never yellow. Most have a strong, fruity scent. The heterogeneous mixture of crossings that produced them is so complex that it is almost impossible to recognize the characters of the various sections involved. *Rosa gallica*, or alternatively *Rosa damascena*, may be responsible for the fragrance, *Rosa* × *centifolia* for the shape of the flowers with their large petals, *Rosa* × *borboniana* and the Tea Roses for their remontant qualities. They were also hybridized among themselves, resulting in the breeding of a great many Hybrid Perpetuals in the middle of the nineteenth century (thirty or forty new varieties a year), although many have disappeared today, perhaps partly because of fashion, and probably also because these roses are very prone to fungal diseases.

The Hybrid Teas have a very complex genealogy because they are the result of a combination of all the rose sections. They have also been frequently hybridized among themselves. Their flowers are in the classic style that we all instantly conjure up when thinking of a rose, with a pointed centre, backward-curving exterior petals, and a fruity fragrance. 'Étoile de Hollande' is an excellent and strongly scented variety, much less rigid in appearance than those roses in this group that, since the mid-twentieth century, have constituted almost all the roses grown under glass for sale as cut flowers. The history of the Hybrid Tea varieties shows that breeders have, unfortunately, preferred the shape and size of the flower to its beauty and scent, making the rose into a standardized commercial product.

Some sections native to China

The Banksiae

This section consists of *Rosa banksiae* and its hybrids. They are climbers with abundant foliage and prefer a temperate climate. From the first fine days of April *Rosa banksiae lutea*, which is completely thornless, adorns walls and arbours in such mild areas of France as Provence and the Côte d'Azur with clusters of small, pale yellow flowers. The main stem, which sheds its bark in strips, can sometimes grow as large in diameter as a tree trunk.

The Laevigatae

Rosa laevigata and its hybrids have glossy, semi-evergreen leaves consisting of only three leaflets. The shrubs bear large, white, single flowers which are spectacular in May. The bristly fruits are very ornamental. Although these shrubs are not very widely grown, they will do well in a sheltered place.

The Bracteatae

Rosa bracteata, discovered in China in 1795, is a beautiful sight with its rounded leaflets and white flowers, borne in summer with intermittent repeat flowerings until autumn. It has two hybrids, one of which, 'Mermaid', with large yellow flowers, is much more robust in appearance than the type,* and is popular with many rose-lovers.

Left and facing page

Rosa chinensis 'Général Shablikine' (× 2.30 and × 1.5)

The subgenus Platyrhodon

Rosa roxburghii and its hybrids are classified separately from other roses. The species is the only one in the Platyrhodon subgenus. It is unusual in every way: it has fern-like foliage, flowers with crumpled petals, green fruits with stiff bristles, and bark which flakes away, becoming white and smooth. The first shrub found in 1824, *Rosa roxburghii* 'Roxburghii', has very double, remontant, deep pink flowers, while *Rosa roxburghii* 'Normalis', discovered in 1908, has single, pale pink flowers and is not remontant.

This survey, which is not exhaustive, gives some idea of the riches of the rose world and the extent of its genetic roots. The physical roots of roses can also reach a long way when they have to penetrate stony soil, drawing nourishment from lower and lower down – a rose naturalized in this way can live for over a century. The Hildesheim Rose of Germany, said to date from the time of Charlemagne's son and therefore to be a thousand years old, is often mentioned as an example of great age. However, such ancient rose bushes seldom survive. Some of the species roses in the gardens of L'Haÿ-les-Roses in France are centenarians; they are magnificent specimens. Unless you have seen them it is hard to imagine the sense of strength and vitality they convey. Their hardy, robust qualities and ability to adapt to circumstances are astonishing.

Old roses are dispersed over a very wide area, but we grow only a small selection of varieties in our gardens by comparison with the great diversity of the entire range.

The history of rose-growing

The first gardens were made in the Middle East, around the Persian Gulf, created in the desert about six hundred years before Christ. Irrigation gave them wonderful fertility, producing colourful fruits and flowers.

In the West, the Romans grew whole fields of roses for the sake of their petals. They sprinkled rose petals on the couches where they reclined to eat their meals, the beds where they slept, and their funeral biers. Another Roman custom was to shower military conquerors or guests at a banquet with rose petals.

Since the rose was the favourite flower of Venus, the goddess of love and beauty, the early Christians regarded it as a pagan symbol. Then they too were gradually won over, and made it the flower of the Virgin Mary. Charlemagne initiated the custom of planting roses near religious buildings, and the monks undertook to maintain them. Despite these first attempts at gardening, however, ornamental gardens were not really introduced to the West until the Renaissance.

The rose was still reserved for a prosperous élite: the clerics who grew roses on their land, the courtiers who liked its fragrance. The Provins region of France, close to the capital, was famous for its intensive growing of *Rosa gallica officinalis*, the 'Apothecary's Rose' or 'Provins Rose', from which rose-water was extracted.

Since the rose was so popular at court, naturally enough it was despised during the French Revolution. The history of the 'Chevette Rose', as told by Abel Belmont in his late nineteenth-century *Dictionnaire historique et artistique de la rose*, is a poignant example. During the reign of Louis XVI, a rose-grower called Chevet lived in the village of Bagnolet. He was famous for his breeding of new roses, one of which bore his name and was known as the 'Chevette Rose'. However, the Revolution came, and with it disaster. Monsieur Chevet was accused of plotting to help Queen Marie-Antoinette escape: he had passed her a note through her prison bars, hidden in a bunch of roses. He was condemned to death by the Revolutionary tribunal, which said, however, that it would grant him a last wish. Monsieur Chevet asked for one or all of the members of the tribunal to bring up the seventeen children who would be left destitute at his death. After some deliberation, the tribunal agreed to spare the life of the father of such a large family, but on condition that he rooted out all his rose bushes and never again grew anything but potatoes to feed the people. And that was the end of the 'Chevette Rose'.

When France was at peace once more, under the First Empire, the Empress Josephine, who was born in Martinique, married Napoleon, and was later divorced from him, made the first great garden collection of roses. She sent to Holland and England for rose varieties, in order to assemble as many as possible in her rose garden. With the help of the rose-grower André Du Pont, she acquired two hundred and fifty, and many horticulturalists were inspired to emulate her. In 1805 Josephine recruited the services of the painter Pierre-Joseph Redouté, who spent seven years producing his three-volume masterpiece entitled *Les Roses.*

The imagination of growers and breeders was given full rein during the nineteenth century, stimulated by the finds of famous travellers, and rose gardens became an important element of horticulture. Landscape gardens in both the French and the English manner had fine collections during this period. Breeders worked with enthusiasm in pursuit of style and fashion, and a great many new roses were created. Around the turn of the century, the rose broke down social barriers and came to be grown in kitchen gardens, looking even more decorative around cottages than in the grounds of castles, and today almost every small garden has its roses.

Travelling botanists

Our gardens would be much the poorer without the attractive and exotic plants raised from seeds and cuttings of all kinds brought back by travellers. *Rosa gallica officinalis,* the 'Apothecary's Rose', came from Syria to France on horseback with Count Thibaut of Champagne in the thirteenth century. Early in the nineteenth century, John Parks brought *Rosa* × *odorata ochroleuca* ('Parks' Yellow Tea-Scented China') to England from China by sedan-chair and on board ship. Similarly, Robert Fortune discovered 'Fortune's Double Yellow', and brought it back to Europe. Roses from China crossed the Indian Ocean and stopped off at the Ile de la Réunion, then the Ile de Bourbon, where the colonists planted them as hedges. They crossed with each other, and hybridized with *Rosa damascena,* the 'Quatre Saisons' rose, to produce the first Bourbon Roses. A Monsieur Bréon noticed them, and they were sent (perhaps by post?) to Paris, where Louis Philippe's gardener Monsieur Jacques succeeded in breeding descendants. A lengthy exchange of seeds between the Noisette brothers led to the introduction of the 'Blush Noisette' variety, bred in America and sent back to Europe.

Roses reached France from all over Asia, particularly Japan, where *Rosa multiflora* and *Rosa rugosa* were discovered at just the right time to be used in the hybridization process by such inspired rose-growers as Cochet and Gravereaux. They then spread to the rest of Europe and the United States. We thus have a great many roses native to various different countries, and often bearing the names of their discoverers (for instance, the French priest Father Soulié is commemorated in the name of *Rosa soulieana,* Madame Fedtschenko in the name of *Rosa fedtschenkoana*). Today roses travel by train and plane, finding their way into the baggage and the pockets of enthusiastic rose-lovers, to such an extent and so successfully that many countries, including those of the southern hemisphere (the biggest rose garden in the world is at the Cape), have acclimatized thousands of varieties.

Rose-growing families and their roses

The beauty and diversity of wild roses have always delighted us, but do not satisfy our insatiable desire for change. The breeder takes pleasure in manipulating forms by artificial hybridization, depositing pollen collected from the stamens of one variety on the shiny stigmata* of another. His skill lies in choosing the parents most likely to produce a good result. The seeds thus formed are then sown, and plants are selected according to the breeder's criteria. The entire process takes several years. Enthusiastic rose-breeders have often been members of successive generations of the same family, with fathers passing down to their sons

Above

Rosa × centifolia muscosa 'Mme Louis Lévêque' (× 1)

the preliminary results of promising but unfinished work.

The first great rose show was held at Lyons in 1845. For rose-growers, it became an annual opportunity to display their best new roses. Like artists, each of these pioneers of plant genetics had his own style and field of special interest. In France, the Guillot family worked with Tea Roses and bred the first Polyantha. The Pernet-Duchers concentrated on creating remontant yellow roses, starting out from *Rosa foetida*, and in 1908 they bred 'Rayon d'Or' (no longer grown today). The Nabonnands of Golfe-Juan gave us some magnificent copper-tinted roses descended from *Rosa chinensis*; other French families of rose-breeders have included the Moreau-Roberts, the Viberts, the Chedannes, the Verdiers, and the Gravereaux family, who created an outstanding rose collection at L'Haÿ-les-Roses. English rose-breeders have included Henry Bennet, and at the beginning of the twentieth century the Reverend Joseph Pemberton and his associates, who created the revolutionary Hybrid Musk group of roses. The Ketten brothers worked in Luxembourg, the Dicksons and McGredys grew roses in Ireland, the firm of Jackson and Perkins in the USA, and the Petersen and Poulsen rose nurseries were Danish. In Germany, the Kordes family has left such a mark on modern horticulture that a new species bred by them, the origin of a whole new group, was named *Rosa kordesii.* With the firm of Kordes, however, we come to modern times. Rose-breeders are still exploring the past, in search of wonders as yet unknown, in order to create new roses.

The rose, mankind's companion

The rose symbolizes perfection of shape. Rose windows, an architectural feature in the shape of a full-blown rose, give structural form to the stained glass of our finest Gothic cathedrals. The rose has inspired many nature painters, notably the Dutch artist Jan Van Huysum (1682–1749), the Belgian Pierre-Joseph Redouté (1759–1840) – sometimes called the "Raphael of flowers" – who was in the service successively of Queen Marie-Antoinette and the Empresses Josephine and Marie-Louise, and the French painter Henri Fantin-Latour (1836–1904), whose name has been given to one of the best varieties of *Rosa × centifolia* (of unknown origin).

A very adaptable plant, the rose has always fascinated botanists, who have taken a keen interest in propagating it and selecting its mutations. Its wonderful scent has always been highly prized, and fields of roses are still cultivated.

Grown under glass for sale as cut flowers, modern roses have been selected to answer commercial requirements, and it is very difficult to buy an old rose at a florist's shop: the moss rose, for instance, is unknown to the trade. But whatever happens to the rose, the symbol remains intact. Will future generations succeed in preserving the lovely and much-travelled queen of flowers, fascinating in her variety, and still a source of exquisite pleasure?

Symbolism and poetry

Oh, no man knows
Through what wild centuries
Roves back the rose.
Walter de la Mare, *All That's Past*

The symbolism of the rose is present in classical mythology. Cupid covers the bed on which Mars and Venus make love with roses. According to Virgil, Venus had a rosy neck and Achilles a rosy hand. The ancient Greeks wore crowns of roses at banquets, and a bride entered her husband's house wearing a rose wreath. In Roman festivals, the rose took on a sacred, purifying character, and the tale of Lucius describes the hero of the story triumphing over his cruel fate thanks to roses. Changed into a donkey after a series of misfortunes, he regains his own shape during a street theatre performance: "At that moment a man carrying flowers passed by. I saw that there were freshly gathered rose leaves [petals] among them. Without hesitating for a moment, I jumped off the couch and ran to the flowers. My audience thought I was getting up to dance, but I looked through all the flowers in turn, picked out the roses and ate them. While the spectators were still watching in amazement, my beast-like form faded and fell away, the donkey was no more, and the Lucius concealed within my skin appeared, standing upright like a man." (Lucian of Samosata [attrib.], *Lucius* or *The Ass*, second century AD).

Ornamental plants were not widely grown in Europe during the Middle Ages, but the rose was highly regarded in the Middle East, and was central to Persian mystical poetry. In the West, the Renaissance and later centuries brought a liberalization of ideas. The rose as a symbol of love was dedicated to women, and much used in poetic language to suggest the transience of beauty:

Gather ye rosebuds while ye may,
Old Time is still a-flying:
And this same flower that smiles today,
Tomorrow will be dying.
Robert Herrick, *To Virgins, to Make Much of Time*

The rose was already being used to adorn tombs in ancient Egypt at the time of the Pharaohs. This seems to have become a standard practice, continuing to the present day, for there are rose bushes of considerable age growing in cemeteries all over Europe. The rose was chosen above all other flowers to transcend death:

Strew on her roses, roses,
And never a spray of yew.
In quiet she reposes:
Ah! would that I did too.
Matthew Arnold, *Requiescat*

Singers and poets still write about roses, and the rose invites us to dream in our gardens. Anyone who once planted a rose now grown into a splendid shrub will have a very special place in our hearts, for the gardener's art calls for both skill and strong motivation. A rose planted near the family home may mark a significant date in the lives of our forebears, and its mere fragrance will bring back memories.

Everyday pleasures

Bouquets and flower arrangements

A bouquet or flower arrangement is the essence of the garden, embodying the sense of wonder it conveys, a wonder we wish to preserve and share. Although florists can create very handsome bouquets with hothouse flowers, garden flowers make versatile arrangements: warm, vibrant, and beautifully scented. Moreover, they are the result of our own labours – our harvest. All old rose varieties look pretty in a vase. Single roses, double roses, and clusters of roses are all suitable and will not lose their petals too quickly. You can mingle several varieties when you cut them, leaving a good amount of foliage on the stems. Old roses go well together, and there is no need for long, straight stems or any particular skill in flower arranging. The best bouquets fall into shape as they are cut and held in the hand, and can be put in a vase just as they are. You can add perennial flowers and grasses to lighten the general effect, enhance the colours, or introduce a touch of blue.

Roses picked in bud early in the morning will open indoors and last longer than flowers picked fully blown, but they will not have such a strong scent. Put a bunch of roses in a cool room where it will not be in the sun for more than an hour or so during the day. That brief period of sunlight is a wonderful experience; the heat of the sun falling on the flowers will release their fragrance, and if you then shut the door the whole room will smell of roses for hours. You can repeat the process every day for up to a week.

A very pretty table decoration can be made by floating the heads of roses on the surface of water in small glass bowls, which can be passed from hand to hand. Or you can cut roses in bud to use in a casual display.

Pot-pourri

To make pot-pourri, fill a jar with alternate layers of coarse salt and dried rose petals, with or without other flowers or pieces of bark. Fill the jar gradually, taking care to keep it covered. Leave to mature for a month or two. A few drops of essence of roses will revive the scent.

Roses in the kitchen

Although the rose itself has no special medicinal properties, its fruits contain a good deal of vitamin C.
INFUSIONS
In winter, rose-hip tea made with the fruits of the dog rose, *Rosa canina*, is good for infections. The taste is pleasant and slightly acid. Seven or eight crushed hips will make two cups.
ROSE HONEY
Simmer 100 g (4 oz) of eucalyptus or pine honey and 50 g (2 oz) of red Provins rose petals (*Rosa officinalis*) for about ten minutes. Put through a sieve and pour into jars. A small spoonful of rose honey melted in the mouth is good for sore throats and a hoarse voice.
ROSE PETAL JELLY
'Rose de Rescht' or *Rosa* × *centifolia major* are perfect for this recipe.
Take 500 g (1 lb) rose petals, 1/2 litre (1 pt) water, 750 g (1 1/2 lb) sugar lumps, 10 cl (4 fl oz) water, the juice of two lemons, two or three spoonfuls of rose-water (optional). You may have to use a little pectin if the jelly does not set easily. After removing the white bases (ungues) of the petals, wash and drain them. Steep them in 1/2 litre (1 pt) cold water for twelve hours. Boil the sugar with 10 cl (4 fl oz) water in a preserving pan. When the surface is covered with large bubbles, add the petals with the water in which they have been soaking, and the lemon juice. Boil for 30 minutes, testing for a set now and then. Pour into jars.
CRYSTALLIZED ROSE PETALS
A very pretty and delicious decoration.
Beat one egg white, two spoonfuls of water and a few drops of rose-water in a bowl. Using a brush, coat whole fresh rose petals thinly with this mixture. Dust with sugar over a plate and place carefully on a wire rack. When they are dry, crisp and stiff, store in a tin between layers of greaseproof paper.
ROSE SYRUP
To make 1 litre (2 pts): 300 g (12 oz) fresh rose petals (e.g. 'Rose de Rescht', *Rosa* × *centifolia*, *Rosa damascena*), 40 cl (1/2 pt) spring water, 2 kg (4 lb) sugar, 40 cl (1/2 pt) distilled rose-water.

Put the petals in the water, cover, and leave to steep for twenty-four hours. Filter. Heat gently and add the sugar and distilled rose-water, without stirring. Bring to the boil, watching all the time. Take the pan off the stove as soon as the syrup boils, or it will rise and overflow. Pour into bottles and seal hermetically. If the syrup looks too pale, you can add a few drops of beetroot juice or cochineal.

The rose in perfumery

Distilled rose-water is an astringent lotion and feels delicious patted on the face when you wake up. Essence of roses, an oily, concentrated substance steam-extracted from the flowers of *Rosa damascena* 'Kazanlik', is produced by a second distillation process. The method is thought to have been discovered in Persia in the fourteenth century, and then dispersed by the Arabs. It takes an enormous quantity of roses to make a tiny amount of essence. In the valley of Dadès in Morocco many families make a living from selling rose petals; rose-growing is a cottage industry here, with its own traditional festivals. In Bulgaria and Turkey, however, roses are grown on an industrial scale, calling for a large labour force picking in the fields from sunrise. Essence of roses, being rare and expensive, is much sought after and is kept for export. It is used in the blending of luxury perfumes, although today it has to compete with synthetic essences which threaten intensive rose-growing of this kind.

At Grasse in France, a very few perfume-makers still use 'Rose de Mai', a hybrid produced by crossing *Rosa × centifolia* with *Rosa gallica.*

The History of the Republic of Roses

"A wise man has said: happy is the man without ambition. I would add, happy too is the modest, well-informed enthusiast who, like you, Monsieur Gravereaux, limits his ambition to inscribing his name in a useful and delightful chapter of the History of the Republic of Roses." It was in these terms that Monsieur Vigier, then Minister of Agriculture in France, addressed Jules Gravereaux, the first great collector of roses in his gardens of L'Haÿ-les-Roses, in the year 1900. By the "Republic of Roses" he meant the genus Rosa as a whole, implying that every rose still extant should now be in the public domain. The adventures of these roses through recorded history could almost make us forget that they are merely plants.

The intricate reconstruction of the genetic origin of old varieties has now become a subject of scientific research that may or may not solve the riddles of their parentage. It hardly matters to an enthusiast if old roses speak their own secret language, which does not really need to be deciphered. We can discover roses one by one, examining them carefully, breathing in their fragrance. We hold the frail flowers in our fingertips, and their meaning is suddenly clear.

Above

Rosa multibracteata (× 1.25)

Left

Rosa rubiginosa (× 1)

Synonyms: 'Eglantine Rose', 'Sweet Briar', 'Rosier Rouillé'. With *Rosa canina*, this is one of the most common species roses found growing wild. It differs from *Rosa canina* in the deeper pink of its flowers, and is easily identified by the green apple scent of its crumpled leaves. It likes chalky soils.
Shrub: 2.5 × 1.5 m (8 1/4 × 5 ft). Full sun. Diameter of flowers: 3 cm (1 1/4 in), 5 petals. Fruits. Scent***. Not remontant.

Right

Rosa rubrifolia

'Sir Cedric Morris' (× 0.27)

Found by Sir Cedric Morris in 1979 and introduced by Peter Beales, this rose is probably a spontaneous hybrid of *Rosa rubrifolia* and *Rosa mulliganii*. It is one of the fastest-growing of all ramblers,* scrambling from tree to tree. Its large clusters of flowers are followed by orange hips, creating an attractive effect against the dull, purplish foliage.
Rambler: 10 m (33 ft) or more. Partial shade. Diameter of flowers: 3 cm (1 1/4 in), 5 petals. Decorative fruits. Scent*. Not remontant.

Facing page

Rosa × alba

'Cuisse de Nymphe' (× 1.25)

Synonym: 'Maiden's Blush', referring to the flower's colour (resembling the blushing cheeks of a modest girl). The French name means 'Nymph's Thigh'. This is probably the best-known of all old roses because of its name and its beauty, although it is not very widely grown. According to the documentary records, it has been in cultivation since at least 1550.
Shrub: 2 × 1.5 m (6 1/2 × 5 ft). Full sun or partial shade. Diameter of flowers: 8 cm (3 in), over 40 petals. Scent***. Not remontant.

Below

Rosa × *alba*

'Reine du Danemark' (× 1.14)

Synonyms: 'Königin von Dänemark', 'Queen of Denmark', 'New Maiden's Blush', 'Naissance de Vénus'. Bred by Booth in 1816, this rose may have grown from a seed of 'Cuisse de Nymphe', or alternatively may be the result of crossing *Rosa alba* with *Rosa damascena*. It has greyish-green foliage, and bears beautiful flowers in June; they are pure pink, deeper at the heart, and perfectly shaped. The incurved petals form an elaborate rosette, and are beautifully scented.
Shrub: 1.8 × 1.3 m (6 × 4 1/4 ft). Full sun or partial shade. Diameter of flowers: 8 cm (3 in), over 40 petals. Scent***. Not remontant.

Facing page

Rosa × *alba*

'Félicité Parmentier' (× 8)

Bred by Parmentier in 1835. The cream-coloured buds, round and tightly packed, open to show pale pink flowers. One of the most strongly scented of all old roses.
Shrub: 1.5 × 1.2 m (5 × 4 ft). Full sun or partial shade. Diameter of flowers: 6 cm (2 1/2 in), over 40 petals. Scent***. Not remontant.

Below and facing page

Rosa omeiensis chrysocarpa

(× 1.60 and × 2.60)

Originally from Sichuan in China, this remarkably vigorous shrub is famous for its extremely decorative, large, blood-red, translucent thorns. Its flowers have four petals of a soft white shade, very pretty and fragrant, arranged all along the stems. Should be planted to be seen against the light so that the thorns are effectively displayed.
Shrub: 3 × 3 m (10 × 10 ft). Diameter of flowers: 3 cm (1 1/4 in), 4 petals. Yellow fruits. Scent**. Not remontant.

Right

Rosa xanthina

(× 0.70)

Found in the wild in China, Mongolia, and Turkestan. It has small leaves, red stems, and yellow flowers. It can be confused with 'Canary Bird', which it closely resembles. Flowering is early and prolonged, sometimes from the beginning of April until June. Its graceful habit of growth is very decorative.
Shrub: 2.5 × 2 m (8 1/4 × 6 1/2 ft). Full sun or partial shade. Diameter of flowers: 5 cm (2 in), 5 petals. Not remontant.

Above

Rosa pernettiana

'Rhodophile Gravereaux' (× 1.05)

Right

Rosa pimpinellifolia

'Single Cherry' (× 1)

Bred in 1900 by Pernet-Ducher from *Rosa foetida* (a yellow-flowered wild rose widely found in Asia), this shrub has almost disappeared from our gardens. It flowers early in May, with very beautiful blooms of an unusual orange-yellow with a touch of pink. Unfortunately, it is prone to suffer from black spot.
Shrub: 1.5 × 1.3 m (5 × 4 1/4 ft). Sun or partial shade; well-drained soil. Diameter of flowers: 8 cm (3 1/4 in), 5–10 petals. Not remontant.

Below

Rosa pimpinellifolia

'Single Cherry' (× 5.4)

Introduced by Kordes, but of unknown origin, this shrub has dark foliage, with small but abundant leaves, and cherry-red flowers with a paler underside to the petals. The habit of growth is attractive and compact, with good growth. Autumn enhances the colour of the foliage, turning it coppery, while the round fruits are black.
Shrub: 1.5 × 1.5 m (5 × 5 ft). Full sun.
Diameter of flowers: 5 cm (2 in), 5 petals.
Fruits. Not remontant.

Above

Rosa nitida

'Dart's Defender' (× 1.5)

A cross between *Rosa nitida* and *Rosa rugosa* 'Hansa', bred by Monsieur Dart's Huis in 1971, and particularly successful because it retains the good qualities of both parents. Its scented flowers last a long time. The foliage turns from dark green to purplish-orange in autumn (and is very useful in arrangements). It throws up suckers.
Shrub: 1.5 × 1.5 m (5 × 5 ft). Sun or partial shade. Diameter of flowers: 7 cm (2 ³/₄ in), 20–40 petals. Fruits. Scent**. Not remontant.

Above

Rosa farreri persetosa (× 1.65)

Seeds brought back from China in 1915 by Reginald Farrer grew into young plants, and E.A. Bowles selected this rose, also known as the 'Threepenny Bit Rose' because of its miniature leaflets. The buds and flowers are surprisingly small in view of the shrub's impressive size. The stems are covered with fine thorns, the habit of growth is elegant, and the whole plant has an airy lightness.
Shrub: 2 × 3 m (6 1/2 × 10 ft). Partial shade.
Diameter of flowers: 1.5 cm (3/4 in), 5 petals.
Not remontant.

Above and facing page

Rosa moyesii (× 1 and × 2.19)

Discovered in western China in 1890, this is a magnificent wild rose with carmine flowers set off by golden-bronze stamens. Its habit of growth is tall and erect, and the foliage consists of many small, round leaflets. This is one of the most spectacular of species roses. Its long, bottle-shaped hips provide a feast for birds. Very frost-hardy.
Large shrub or climber: 3.5 × 3 m (11 $^1/_2$ × 10 ft) or more. Full sun or partial shade. Diameter of flowers: 6 cm (2 $^1/_2$ in), 5 petals. Fruits. Not remontant.

Right

Rosa fedtschenkoana (× 1.9)

Discovered in the mountains of Asia by the Fedtschenkos around 1871 and taken to the gardens of St Petersburg, this is one of the few species roses to be intermittently repeat-flowering from June to the first frosts. Its feathery foliage is light grey-green. It puts up suckers.
Shrub: 2.5 × 2 m (8 1/4 × 6 1/2 ft). Full sun.
Diameter of flowers: 4 cm (1 1/2 in), 5 petals.

Below

Rosa × micrugosa

'Walter Butt' (× 2)

A hybrid of *Rosa rugosa* and *Rosa roxburghii* bred by Butt in 1954. It has translucent, very pure pale pink flowers, followed by bristly orange hips like the fruits of *Rosa roxburghii.*
Shrub: 2.5 × 2 m (8 1/4 × 6 1/2 ft). Full sun or partial shade. Diameter of flowers: 9 cm (3 1/2 in), 5 petals. Not remontant.

Below

Rosa rugosa

'Roseraie de L'Haÿ' (× 1)

Bred by Cochet-Cochet in 1901, this is a superb variety, with loosely structured double blooms rather like a peony. They are strongly scented, with a peppery fragrance, deep carmine pink, and repeat-flower well until the end of summer. The habit of growth of the adult plant is arching and parasol-shaped. It will grow well in chalky soil. For hedges or flower-beds, but particularly attractive grown as a specimen shrub.
Shrub: 2 × 1.6 m (6 1/2 × 5 1/4 ft). Full sun or partial shade. Diameter of flowers: 9 cm (3 1/2 in), 20–40 petals. Scent***.

Facing page

Rosa rugosa

'Frau Dagmar Hastrup' (× 1.9)

Bred by Hastrup in 1914. It makes an undemanding compact bush, with single flowers until the first frosts. The globular fruits, like little tomatoes, form while the plant is still flowering, providing a very decorative effect. The foliage is crinkled and turns mustard yellow in autumn. Good in hilly areas.
Bush: 1.3 × 1.2 m (4 1/4 × 4 ft). Full sun. Diameter of flowers: 7 cm (2 3/4 in), 5 petals. Fruits. Scent*.

Above

Rosa rugosa

'Villa des Tybilles' (× 0.7)

Bred by Jules Gravereaux at L'Haÿ-les-Roses in 1899. This rose is hardly ever seen in gardens today, perhaps because it is not remontant. However, it is a very attractive shrub with its bright red flowers, golden stamens, unusual foliage, and interesting name.
Shrub: 2 × 1.5 m (6 $^{1}/_{2}$ × 5 ft). Full sun.
Diameter of flowers: 7 cm (2 $^{3}/_{4}$ in), 5 petals.
Fruits. Scent**. Not remontant.

Left and facing page

Rosa rugosa

'Scabrosa' (× 1.28)

An opulent rose of unknown parentage. Its vigorous branches bear broad, luxuriant, crinkled foliage. Its deep pink and very fragrant flowers appear throughout the summer and are followed by large clusters of hips. It throws up suckers.
Shrub: 2 × 1.8 m (6 $^{1}/_{2}$ × 6 ft). Full sun.
Diameter of flowers: 12 cm (4 $^{3}/_{4}$ in), 5 petals. Fruits. Scent**.

Facing page

Rosa × centifolia

'Cristata' (× 1.29)

Synonyms: 'Chapeau de Napoléon', 'Crested Moss'. Bred by Vibert in 1827. In hot weather this rose has a strong, heady scent. It is very like *Rosa centifolia major*, but with a feature of its own which makes it instantly recognizable: the sepals are broad and heavily mossed. Its habit of growth is arching.
Vigorous shrub: 1.5 × 1.5 m (5 × 5 ft). Full sun. Diameter of flowers: 8 cm (3 1/4 in), over 40 petals. Scent***. Not remontant.

Above

Rosa gallica (× 1)

This wild rose grows in the Hautes-Alpes, where it is a protected plant. When grown in enriched soil, it is not unusual to see its luminous corolla* add another row of petals and become semi-double.
Bush, producing suckers: 1 × 1 m (3 1/4 × 3 1/4 ft). Full sun. Diameter of flowers: 6 cm (2 1/2 in), 5 petals. Scent**. Not remontant.

Facing page

Rosa × *centifolia*

'Fantin-Latour' (× 1.54)

Little is known about the origin of this rose, except that it was called after the French flower painter and has won the title of Best Garden Rose. Its foliage resembles that of a China Rose. The flower, flesh-pink with a deeper centre, has the voluptuous look of a peony. A very vigorous rose with a long flowering season.
Dense shrub: 1.5 × 1.5 m (5 × 5 ft). Full sun or partial shade. Diameter of flowers: 9 cm (3 1/2 in), over 40 petals. Scent**. Not remontant.

Right

Rosa × *centifolia*

'Juno' (× 0.7)

Bred by Laffay in 1847, this rose bends under the weight of its globular flowers, which are very large, silvery pink in colour, and a slightly deeper pink at the edges, contrasting with the deep, dull green of the leaves. Although little grown, 'Juno' is a spectacular rose.
Arching bush: 1.4 × 1.2 m (4 1/2 × 4 ft). Full sun. Diameter of flowers: 10 cm (4 in), over 40 petals. Scent***. Not remontant.

Facing page, above

Rosa × *centifolia*

'Petite Lisette' (× 0.63)

Vibert bred this beautiful little rose in 1817. Small and fine-textured, the rose-pink petals are regularly incurved to the centre. The flat, perfectly circular flowers are elegantly borne all over the plant.
Bush: 1.4 × 1.2 m (4 ½ × 4 ft). Full sun or partial shade. Diameter of flowers: 6 cm (2 ½ in), over 40 petals. Scent***. Not remontant.

Left

Rosa × *centifolia major* (× 1.25)

Synonym: 'Rose des Peintres'. This famous rose of unknown origin was one of those most frequently planted in early twentieth-century gardens, where it can still be found growing vigorously even when neglected. Its flowers are of the deeply cupped, globular "cabbage rose" shape popular with eighteenth-century Dutch painters, and its strong scent lingers in the memory.
Arching shrub: 2 × 1.8 m (6 ½ × 6 ft). Full sun. Diameter of flowers: 9 cm (3 ½ in), over 40 petals. Scent***. Not remontant.

Below

Rosa × centifolia muscosa alba

(× 0.62)

Synonyms: 'Mousseuse Blanche', 'Shailer's White Moss'. This mutation of *Rosa × centifolia muscosa* appeared in England in 1788. Strongly scented, the very pale pink flowers are surrounded by mossy sepals full of resinous sap. Vigorous shrub: 1.8 × 1.2 m (6 × 4 ft). Full sun (to bring out the fragrance). Diameter of flowers: 8 cm (3 $^{1}/_{4}$ in), over 40 petals. Scent***. Not remontant.

Right and above

Rosa × centifolia muscosa

'Béranger' (× 1.16 and × 1.14)

Bred by Vibert in 1849, this rose is no longer grown in our gardens. The pink flowers with their incurving petals are borne on stems with fine thorns. The shrub is vigorous.
Shrub: 1.5 × 1 m (5 × 3 1/4 ft). Full sun. Diameter of flowers: 6 cm (2 1/2 in), 20–40 petals. Scent**. Not remontant.

Facing page

Rosa × centifolia muscosa

'Alfred de Dalmas' (× 2.51)

Synonym: 'Mousseline'. Bred by Portemer in 1855, this rose bears fine silvery white, cup-shaped flowers, with an open centre exposing the stamens. It is lightly mossed, and there are few thorns on the stems. It repeat-flowers well, and throws up suckers.
Bush: 90 × 80 cm (3 × 2 3/4 ft). Full sun. Diameter of flowers: 7 cm (2 3/4 in), 20–40 petals. Scent*.

Below

Rosa × *centifolia muscosa*

'Henri Martin' (× 0.62)

Synonym: 'Red Moss'. Bred by Laffay, this rose has stems, buds, and fruits covered with straight bristles rather than moss. The blooms, which are an unusual bright red, resist wet weather well. Not a demanding rose.
Bush: 1.5 × 1 m (5 × 3 1/4 ft). Full sun or partial shade. Diameter of flowers: 8 cm (3 1/4 in), 10–20 petals. Fruits. Scent***. Not remontant.

Right

Rosa × *centifolia muscosa*

'Eugénie Guinoisseau' (× 0.62)

Bred by Guinoisseau in 1864, this upright shrub bears large, bright cherry-red flowers. The "moss" on the foliage and buds is deep and almost metallic in colour. After the abundant June flowering, blooms appear sporadically during summer until autumn.
Bush: 1.5 × 1 m (5 × 3 1/4 ft). Full sun. Diameter of flowers: 8 cm (3 1/4 in), 20–40 petals. Scent***.

Facing page

Rosa × *centifolia muscosa*

'Nuits de Young' (× 2.3)

Synonyms: 'Black Moss', 'Old Black'. Bred by Laffay in 1845, this is an unusual rose with deep, velvety, reddish-purple flowers set off by the golden stamens. The stems and buds are heavily mossed and give a delicious resinous scent. All parts of the plant are dark.
Bush: 1.2 m × 90 cm (4 × 3 ft). Full sun. Diameter of flowers: 5 cm (2 in), 20–40 petals. Scent***. Not remontant.

Above

Rosa × centifolia muscosa

'Salet' (× 0.85)

Facing page

Rosa × centifolia muscosa

'William Lobb' (× 0.92)

Bred by Lacharme in 1854, this undemanding rose produces a generous succession of slightly mossed roses continuously until autumn. The medium-sized flowers, with closely packed, incurving petals, are clear pink and fine-textured. Rain can prevent them from opening properly.
Dense bush: 1.5 × 1.2 m (5 × 4 ft). Full sun. Diameter of flowers: 7 cm (2 3/4 in), over 40 petals. Scent***.

Synonyms: 'Duchesse d'Istrie', 'Old Velvet Moss'. Bred by Laffay in 1855, this heavily mossed rose is interesting for its large dimensions and its colour, violet-purple fading to lilac-grey. It has a tall, arching habit of growth, and it is a good idea to plant perennials at its foot. A very decorative shrub.
Shrub: 1.8 × 1.8 m (6 × 6 ft). Full sun. Diameter of flowers: 8 cm (3 1/4 in), 10–20 petals. Scent***. Not remontant.

Right

Rosa × *damascena*

'Blush Damask' (× 1.32)

A superb old variety; the date of its origin is not known. Pink flowers borne on slightly drooping stems become paler in colour towards the edges and stay on the bush for a long time. There is an indefinable charm about roses such as this, with a history going very far back in time. Bush: 1.2 × 1 m (4 × 3 1/4 ft). Full sun or partial shade. Diameter of flowers: 8 cm (3 1/4 in), 20–40 petals. Scent***. Not remontant.

Facing page

Rosa × *damascena*

'Duchesse de Rohan' (× 1.36)

This rose dates from before 1880, and there is some doubt about its classification. It has some limited repeat-flowering. The cup-shaped blooms are deep pink. It is graceful in habit and, although not widely grown, is a very beautiful variety.
Bush: 1.2 × 1 m (4 × 3 1/4 ft). Full sun. Diameter of flowers: 8 cm (3 1/4 in), 20–40 petals. Scent***.

Above

Rosa × damascena

'Ispahan' (× 1.16)

This rose is mentioned in documentary records before 1832. Although it flowers only once, the bush produces charming pale pink blooms over a long period. Their shape changes as they open fully. The leaves are small and glossy.
Bush: 1.5 × 1 m (5 × 3 1/4 ft). Full sun. Diameter of flowers: 7 cm (2 3/4 in), 10–20 petals. Scent**. Not remontant.

Facing page

Rosa × damascena

'La Ville de Bruxelles' (× 1.35)

Bred by Vibert in 1849, this rose has arching branches and large flowers, flat below but rounded above, pure pink in colour and beautifully shaped. The short petals are incurving towards the centre and attractively arranged.
Arching bush: 1.3 × 1.2 m (4 1/4 × 4 ft). Full sun. Diameter of flowers: 9 cm (3 1/2 in), over 40 petals. Scent***. Not remontant.

Facing page

Rosa × damascena

'Omar Khayyam' (× 1.30)

Introduced in 1893 and planted on Edward Fitzgerald's grave in Suffolk, England, this rose is supposed to come from seeds of roses growing on the tomb of Omar Khayyam in Nashipur in northern Iran. Its beautiful flowers have an intense fragrance in warm weather.
Bush: 1.2 m × 90 cm (4 × 3 ft). Full sun. Diameter of flowers: 8 cm (3 1/4 in), over 40 petals. Scent***. Not remontant.

Left

Rosa × damascena

'Quatre Saisons Blanc Mousseux' (× 1.27)

Synonyms: 'Rosier de Thionville', 'Perpétuelle Mousseuse'. Bred by Laffay in 1835, this rose is likely to be grown only as a curiosity, for its flowering, although remontant, is sparse, and the flowers are rather shapeless. However, its yellowish-grey foliage gives off a remarkable scent and the flowers are beautiful in bud.
Bush: 1.7 × 1.2 m (5 1/2 × 4 ft). Full sun. Diameter of flowers: 7 cm (2 3/4 in), 20–40 petals. Scent*** (foliage).

Facing page

Rosa × damascena

'Rose de Rescht' (× 2.28)

Synonym: *Rosa damascena perpetual.* This rose was brought back from Iran by Nancy Lindsay. It is widely grown in gardens for its many good qualities: ease of cultivation, beauty, and good remontancy. It is also perfect for growing in containers, and is used in confectionery and pot-pourris.

Compact bush: 1.3 × 1 m (4 1/4 × 3 1/4 ft). Full sun. Diameter of flowers: 6 cm (2 1/2 in), over 40 petals. Scent***.

Above

Rosa × damascena

'Rose des Quatre Saisons' (× 0.72)

Synonym: 'The Four Seasons Rose of Paestum'. This very old rose comes from the East, and is thought to have been widely grown by the Romans. It is strongly scented and repeat-flowers until the first frosts. A hardy shrub, its charm lies in the rustic appearance of its pink flowers with their long sepals.

Shrub, easy to maintain: 1.5 × 1.2 m (5 × 4 ft). Full sun. Diameter of flowers: 7 cm (2 3/4 in), 20–40 petals. Scent***.

Facing page

Rosa gallica

'Alain Blanchard' (× 2.42)

Bred by Vibert in 1839, this rose bears semi-double, purple-red flowers smudged with pink and brown and set off by golden stamens. Moderately vigorous, it is not much grown in spite of its beautiful flowers.
Bush: 1.2 × 1 m (4 × 3 ¼ ft). Full sun or partial shade. Diameter of flowers: 8 cm (3 ¼ in), 10–20 petals. Scent**. Not remontant.

Right

Rosa gallica

'Assemblage des Beautés' (× 1.6)

Synonym: 'Rouge Éblouissante'. This rose dates from the end of the eighteenth century, and bears particularly bright and attractive rosette-shaped, cherry-red flowers set off by the dark foliage. A superb rose.
Bush: 1.2 × 1 m (4 × 3 ¼ ft). Full sun or partial shade. Diameter of flowers: 7 cm (2 ¾ in), over 40 petals. Scent**. Not remontant.

Facing page

Rosa gallica

'Belle de Crécy' (× 2.23)

This rose, its breeding attributed to Roeser in 1848, displays the beautiful shades of colour that can occur in the Gallicas, from cherry-red to purplish-pink and turning to lilac as the flowers fade. The petals are incurved towards the centre and show a green eye. Very easy to grow, it has branches with few thorns which can bend under the weight of the large number of its flowers.
Bush: 1.2 × 1 m (4 × $3\frac{1}{4}$ ft). Full sun. Diameter of flowers: 7 cm ($2\frac{3}{4}$ in), over 40 petals. Scent***. Not remontant.

Rosa gallica

'Belle Isis' (× 1)

Bred in Belgium by Parmentier in 1845. The flattened flowers are of medium size, a delicate pale pink, with incurving petals. The habit of growth is erect. The scent of this variety differs from that of other Gallica Roses.
Bush: 1.2 m × 90 cm (4 × 3 ft). Full sun. Diameter of flowers: 6 cm ($2\frac{1}{2}$ in), over 40 petals. Scent*. Not remontant.

Below

Rosa gallica

'Camaïeux' (× 1.90)

Introduced by Vibert in 1830, this rose has flowers in several shades, from pale pink to magenta and greyish-violet, in a particularly fascinating streaked effect. The petals curl and the foliage is slightly pitted, making this an unusual and easily recognized rose.

Bush, moderately vigorous: 1 m × 70 cm (3 1/4 × 2 1/4 ft). Full sun. Diameter of flowers: 8 cm (3 1/4 in), over 40 petals. Scent***. Not remontant.

Below

Rosa gallica

'Cardinal de Richelieu' (× 1.11)

Introduced by Laffay in 1840. A real curiosity, with thin, almost thornless stems and perfectly round buds which open petal by

petal into deep purple flowers with a touch of white. It is rather a delicate rose.
Bush: 1.2 m × 90 cm (4 × 3 ft). Full sun or partial shade. Diameter of flowers: 7 cm (2 3/4 in), over 40 petals. Scent*. Not remontant.

Above

Rosa gallica

'Charles de Mills'

(× 1.8; × 1.8; × 0.5; × 0.5)

Synonym: 'Bizarre Triomphant'. Perhaps the most beautiful of all the Gallica Roses, it is of unknown origin. The Empress Josephine had it in her collection at Malmaison. It has a deep red, flat, perfect corolla with close-packed petals in a quartered arrangement, and an eye in the middle showing the green of the stigmata. Very vigorous.
Shrub, easy to maintain: 1.7 × 1.5 m (5 1/2 × 5 ft). Full sun. Diameter of flowers: 9 cm (3 1/2 in), over 40 petals. Scent***. Not remontant.

Above and left

Rosa gallica

'Charles de Mills'

(× 1.25; × 0.65)

Facing page

Rosa gallica

'Complicata' (× 2)

Thought to be a cross between *Rosa gallica* and *Rosa macrantha.* Not much is known about this rose, which bears little resemblance to other Gallicas, and we may wonder where it gets its name, which is hardly justified. It produces large single flowers of the wild rose type, will grow in any soil, never suffers from disease, and you can do anything you like with it; far from being complicated, it is simplicity itself!
Shrub or climber: 2.5 × 2.5 m (8 1/4 × 8 1/4 ft). Full sun or partial shade, good for hedges. Diameter of flowers: 10 cm (4 in), 5 petals. Fruits. Scent**. Not remontant.

Above

Rosa gallica

'Hippolyte' (× 1)

Of unknown origin, this almost thornless rose produces flattened flowers with the centre, unusually, paler than the edges. The corolla is rich in subtle shades of colour, opening to a particularly beautiful bloom.
Bush: 1.5 × 1 m (5 × 3 1/4 ft). Full sun. Diameter of flowers: 6 cm (2 1/2 in), 20–40 petals. Fruits. Scent**. Not remontant.

Above

Rosa gallica

'Jenny Duval' (× 0.81)

Of unknown origin, dating from the eighteenth century. A typical Gallica in the beautiful colour changes of its petals, which shade from pink to greyish-mauve. It has a long flowering season and is strongly scented.
Bush: 1.3 × 1 m (4 1/4 × 3 1/4 ft). Full sun. Diameter of flowers: 8 cm (3 1/4 in), 20–40 petals. Fruits. Scent***. Not remontant.

Facing page

Rosa gallica

'Louis Van Till' (× 2.13)

This extremely double rose, of unknown parentage, has classic old rose colouring; deeper at the centre of the flower. Grown in full sun it will give off a truly divine fragrance.

Bush: 1.2 m × 90 cm (4 × 3 ft). Full sun. Diameter of flowers: 7 cm (2 3/4 in), over 40 petals. Scent***. Not remontant.

Right

Rosa gallica

'Duchesse de Montebello' (× 0.4)

Of unknown parentage, this superb old rose was introduced in 1826. The buds are slightly tinged with red, and open into flowers of pale pink shading to white; an unusual colour for a Gallica.
Dense bush: 1.2 m × 90 cm (4 × 3 ft). Full sun or partial shade. Diameter of flowers: 7 cm (2 3/4 in), over 40 petals. Scent***. Not remontant.

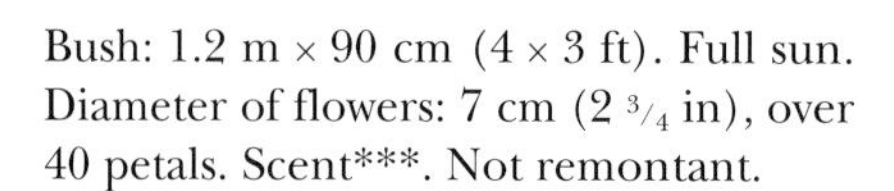

Above

Rosa gallica

'Orpheline de Juillet' (× 1.54)

'July Orphan' seems a strange name for this magnificent dark rose, perhaps with some reference to a survivor of the French Revolution. In any case, the flower and its name are both beautiful, and it also has a wonderful fragrance. Bush: 1.2 m × 90 cm (4 × 3 ft). Full sun. Diameter of flowers: 8 cm (3 1/4 in), over 40 petals. Scent***. Not remontant.

Below

Rosa gallica

'Tuscany' (× 1.3)

Synonym: 'Old Velvet Rose'. The flower is indeed velvety, and of very ancient origin. Golden stamens glow at the heart of the rich, deep purple-red petals. The bush is particularly easy to grow, and the flowers have a strong scent.
Bush: 1 × 1 m (3 1/4 × 3 1/4 ft). Full sun. Diameter of flowers: 6 cm (2 1/2 in), 10–20 petals. Scent***. Not remontant.

Right

Rosa gallica versicolor (× 0.87)

Synonym: 'Rosa Mundi'. Known since the sixteenth century, but probably much older, this rose still has a very contemporary and decorative appearance, with its striped petals and golden-yellow stamens. Bush: 1 × 1 m (3 1/4 × 3 1/4 ft). Full sun. Diameter of flowers: 8 cm (3 1/4 in), 10–20 petals. Fruits. Scent***. Not remontant.

See the bi-coloured rose,
Resembling pearl beneath cornelian
Or two lovers in their retreat,
Lying face to face.

Mondyick
Persian poet, 500 BC

Above

Rosa gallica

'Ville de Londres' (× 0.65)

Bred by Robert in 1850, this rose flowers profusely over a long period. The blooms are bright red, almost luminous, and can bring colour to a flower-bed seen from a distance. Easy to grow. Bush: 1.2 × 1 m (4 × 3 1/4 ft). Full sun. Diameter of flowers: 8 cm (3 1/4 in), over 40 petals. Fruits. Scent***. Not remontant.

Facing page

Rosa gallica

'Violacea' (× 1.2)

Synonyms: 'La Belle Sultane', *Rosa gallica* 'Maheka'. Grown in Holland since 1800, and in the collection at Malmaison. A beautiful shrub all the year round, it will adapt to any soil. The semi-double flowers are purplish-red, set off by a great many yellow stamens. A superb and undemanding rose.

Shrub: 2 × 1.5 m (6 1/2 × 5 ft). Full sun or partial shade. Diameter of flowers: 8 cm (3 1/4 in), 5–10 petals. Fruits. Scent***. Not remontant.

Facing page

Rosa × portlandica

'Jacques Cartier' (× 2.51)

Bred by Moreau-Robert in 1868, this erect bush has pale pink flowers with incurving, perfectly shaped petals emerging from round buds like those of a peony, and nestling in its elongated leaves. It flowers from June to the first frosts and has a delicious scent. Easy to grow, and tolerates hot weather very well.
Bush: 1 m × 80 cm (3 1/4 × 2 3/4 ft), sometimes more. Full sun. Diameter of flowers: 8 cm (3 1/4 in), over 40 petals. Scent***.

Left

Rosa macrantha

'Waitziana' (× 0.55)

Perhaps a hybrid of *Rosa gallica* and *Rosa macrantha*, discovered in France in 1823. The large pale pink flowers produce a great many healthy, long-lasting hips. Prostrate bush: 1 × 1.5 m (3 1/4 × 5 ft). Full sun. Diameter of flowers: 8 cm (3 1/4 in), 5 petals. Fruits. Scent*. Not remontant.

Below

Rosa × portlandica

'Comte de Chambord' (× 1.34)

Bred by Moreau-Robert in 1860. The pink flowers unfurl their petals gracefully. There is good repeat-flowering, and the rose is strongly scented.
Moderately vigorous bush: 1 m × 70 cm (3 1/4 × 2 1/4 ft). Full sun or partial shade. Diameter of flowers: 8 cm (3 1/4 in), over 40 petals. Scent***.

Facing page

Rosa × *portlandica*

'Marbrée' (× 4)

Introduced by Robert and Moreau in 1858. A rather unusual Portland Rose. Its semi-double flowers are strawberry-red smudged with pink, and can sometimes repeat-flower until the end of summer. A vigorous rose.
Bush: 1.2 m × 90 cm (4 × 3 ft). Full sun. Diameter of flowers: 8 cm (3 1/4 in), 10–20 petals. Scent**.

Left

Rosa × *portlandica*

'Yolande d'Aragon' (× 1.1)

Bred by Vibert in 1843, this large, lax bush bears heavy, globular flowers, bright pink and highly scented. The pale green foliage is not very abundant, and the leaflets are long. It is a good idea to plant perennials at its foot, which can look rather bare. Good for cut flowers.
Bush: 1.5 × 1 m (5 × 3 1/4 ft). Full sun or partial shade. Diameter of flowers: 9 cm (3 1/2 in), over 40 petals. Scent***. Remontant.

Above

Rosa sp.

'Betty Sherriff' (× 0.52)

Discovered by Mrs Sherriff in Bhutan, near the Tibetan border, this rose has the luxuriance and glossy foliage of *Rosa mulliganii*, a native of China, although we cannot be sure that they are related. The petals are white tinged with pink, and heart-shaped. Very attractive growth.
Rambler: up to 10 m (33 ft). Full sun or partial shade. Diameter of flowers: 3 cm (1 ¼ in), 5 petals. Fruits. Scent*. Not remontant.

Right

Rosa helenae (× 0.63)

A native of China, and a splendid sight from the moment the first leaves appear. The young shoots are purplish-red, and the leaves have translucent carmine stipules.* The large, scented flower clusters are followed by oval hips. Very vigorous, easy to grow, and hardy.
Rambler: up to 6 m (19 ½ ft) and more. Full sun. Diameter of flowers: 3 cm (1 ¼ in), 5 petals. Fruits. Scent**. Not remontant.

Left

Hybrid Musk

'Cornelia' (× 0.60)

Bred by Pemberton in 1925, this is an excellent variety continuously producing clusters of flowers in pretty, varying shades of coral, yellow, and pink. It never suffers from disease. The long, arched branches bend under the weight of the flowers.
Shrub: 1.5 × 2 m (5 × 6 1/2 ft). Full sun.
Diameter of flowers: 4 cm (1 1/2 in), 20–40 petals. Scent**.

Above

Hybrid Musk

'Nur Mahal' (× 1.30)

Bred by Pemberton in 1923, this rose tolerates hot weather well and is very remontant. It produces clusters of bright, carmine-pink flowers with undulating petals all summer.
Bush: 1.3 × 1 m (4 1/4 × 3 1/4 ft). Full sun.
Diameter of flowers: 8 cm (3 1/4 in), 10–20 petals. Scent*.

Above

Hybrid Musk

'Queen of the Musks' (× 1.30)

Bred by Paul in 1913. Unusual among Hybrid Musks in having compact, well-balanced foliage. Clusters of red buds produce small, pink-tinged flowers fading to white, and the bush is continuous-flowering.
Bush of variable dimensions: 1 to 1.5 × 1.2 m (3 1/4 to 5 × 4 ft). Full sun. Diameter of flowers: 4 cm (1 1/2 in), 10–20 petals. Scent**.

Above

Rosa luciae

'Alexandre Girault' (× 0.33)

Bred by Barbier in 1909. No other rambler has this colouring, in shades of strawberry-red, with incurving petals and a green eye at the centre. The long, flexible stems lend themselves readily to decorative effects (there are fine examples at L'Haÿ-les-Roses).
Rambler: 6 to 10 m (20 to 33 ft). Full sun in an airy situation, or partial shade. Diameter of flowers: 6 cm (2 1/2 in), over 40 petals. Scent*. Not remontant.

Below

Rosa luciae

'François Juranville' (× 0.87)

Bred by Barbier in 1906, from a crossing of *Rosa luciae* and *Rosa chinensis* 'Mme Laurette Messimy'. Exceptionally vigorous, it produces large, pale pink flowers, with deliciously fragrant, incurved central petals. The young shoots are purple. It grows fast and is very healthy.
Rambler: 8 to 13 m (26 to 42 ft). Full sun. Diameter of flowers: 9 cm (3 1/2 in), over 40 petals. Scent***. Not remontant.

Facing page, above

Rosa luciae

'Paul Transon' (× 0.74)

Bred by Barbier in 1900. Very remontant, it produces a cascade of medium-sized, salmon-pink flowers from May until the end of summer, with overlapping petals that scent the air. The leaves are small.
Tall climber: 5 m (16 ft) or more. Full sun or partial shade. Diameter of flowers: 7 cm (2 $^{3}/_{4}$ in), over 40 petals. Scent of green apples***.

Left

Rosa luciae

'Léontine Gervais' (× 1.37)

Bred by Barbier in 1903. Almost as vigorous as 'François Juranville', this variety will rapidly cover pergolas. The highly-scented flowers are semi-double and a pretty orange-pink. Glossy, healthy foliage. Rambler: 6 to 8 m (20 to 26 ft). Full sun or partial shade. Diameter of flowers: 9 cm (3 $^{1}/_{2}$ in), 20–40 petals. Fruits. Scent***. Not remontant.

Facing page

Rosa multiflora inermis (× 1.25)

The multiflora rose, a wild rose of astonishing vigour originating in Japan and Korea, was introduced in 1862. Nurserymen selected its best clones,* including this almost thornless rose, for use as grafting stock on acid soils. The discovery of the species allowed breeders to create many climbers with clusters of small roses and a sweet, fruity fragrance. Shrub: 3 m (10 ft), or grown as a climber to 7 m (23 ft). Full sun or partial shade. Diameter of flowers: 2 cm (3/4 in), 5 petals. Fruits. Scent*. Not remontant.

Above

Rosa multiflora

'Crimson Rambler' (× 0.87)

Imported from Japan, this is thought to be a hybrid of *Rosa wichuraiana* and *Rosa multiflora,* although the theory does not account for the wonderful deep crimson colour of the flowers. It has been unjustly neglected, and remains rare. Almost thornless, it grows very well, despite a slight tendency to suffer from mildew in hot weather.
Rambler: up to 10 m (33 ft). Full sun or partial shade. Diameter of flowers: 3 cm (1 1/4 in), 20–40 petals. Not remontant.

Facing page

Rosa multiflora

'Éléonore Berkeley' (× 0.35)

Of unknown origin, this rose was introduced to continental Europe from England around 1900. It is one of the first roses to flower, with profuse clusters of small, very delicate, lilac-pink blooms. Very vigorous and hardy, although not widely grown.
Climber: 4 × 3 m (13 × 10 ft). Full sun. Diameter of flowers: 3 cm (1 1/4 in), 20–40 petals. Scent**. Not remontant.

Right

Rosa multiflora

'Ghislaine de Féligonde' (× 1.29)

Bred by Turbat in 1916. It bears clusters of small, apricot-yellow flowers which take on a pink tinge and then turn paler. They are sweetly scented and repeat-flower from time to time, with a good autumn flush. An excellent and almost thornless variety that can be grown as a shrub or a climber, and is easy to cultivate.
Specimen shrub, 2.5 × 2.5 m (8 1/4 × 8 1/4 ft), or climber, 3 to 4 m (10 to 13 ft). Full sun or partial shade. Diameter of flowers: 4 cm (1 1/2 in), 20–40 petals. Scent**.

Left

Rosa multiflora

'Veilchenblau' (× 0.75)

Bred by Schmidt in 1909. The colour occurs in no other variety, and looks particularly attractive in partial shade: it is a soft lavender-purple, with white bases to the petals and yellow stamens. The small buds are red. Young, vigorous shoots appear after the flowers, which have a lily-of-the-valley scent.
Climber: 4 to 6 m (13 to 20 ft). Partial shade. Diameter of flowers: 4 cm (1 ½ in), 10–20 petals. Fruits. Scent***. Not remontant.

Facing page

Rosa multiflora

'Laure Davoust' (× 1.20)

Bred by Laffay in 1846. A very attractive rose, with a profusion of lilac-pink pompon-shaped flowers clustering close together, and beautifully scented. The leaves are long and greyish, and the plant is exceptionally vigorous. It sometimes repeat-flowers.
Climber or rambler: 4 to 6 m (13 to 20 ft). Full sun or partial shade. Diameter of flowers: 4 cm (1 ½ in), over 40 petals. Scent***.

Above

Rosa multiflora

'Violette' (× 1.47)

Bred by Turbat in 1921, this rose bears violet-purple flowers of a much deeper shade than 'Veilchenblau'. They are set off by a large quantity of golden stamens, and can be seen from a considerable distance. Very vigorous.
Climber: 2.5 to 4 m (8 1/4 × 13 ft). Full sun or partial shade. Diameter of flowers: 4 cm (1 1/2 in), 5–10 petals. Scent**. Not remontant.

Right

Rose Polyantha

'Mignonnette' (× 0.7)

Bred by Guillot Fils in 1880 from a crossing between *Rosa multiflora* and *Rosa chinensis*, this is a historic rose, being one of the first Polyanthas, along with 'Paquerette'; the latter, however, disappeared. It produces many clusters of charming miniature roses, pale pink in colour and continuing until the first frosts.
Bush: 40 x 30 cm (1 1/4 × 1 ft). Full sun or partial shade. Diameter of flowers: 4 cm (1 1/2 in), 20–40 petals. Scent**.

Below

Rosa sempervirens

'Adélaïde d'Orléans' (× 1.08)

Bred in 1826 by Jacques, gardener to the Duc d'Orléans. Clusters of semi-double flowers, pale pink to white, are borne profusely in June. They have the fresh look of fruit blossom. The foliage is semi-evergreen and growth is luxuriant. Sporadic repeat-flowering sometimes occurs.
Rambler: 3 to 5 m (10 to 16 ft). Full sun or partial shade. Diameter of flowers: 6 cm (2 1/2 in), 10–20 petals. Scent**. Not remontant.

Right

Rosa sempervirens

'Princesse Louise' (× 1.32)

Bred by Jacques in 1829. Cascades of very double, ivory-coloured pompon roses in dense clusters stand out against heavily veined, emerald-green foliage. A healthy, very vigorous rose.
Rambler: up to 5 m (16 ft). Full sun or partial shade. Diameter of flowers: 5 cm (2 in), over 40 petals. Scent*. Not remontant.

Rosa × *wichuraiana*

'Evangéline' (× 0.84)

Bred by Walsh in 1916, this hybrid of *Rosa wichuraiana* and 'Crimson Rambler' is a wonderful rose. An excellent rambler with clusters of white flowers flecked with carmine, which do not open before the end of June, a scent of honeysuckle and remarkable vigour.
Rambler: 5 to 8 m (16 to 26 ft). Full sun or partial shade. Diameter of flowers: 4 cm (1 ½ in), 5 petals. Fruits. Scent***. Not remontant.

Right

Rosa × wichuraiana

'New Dawn' (× 1.2)

Bred by Dreer in 1930, and one of the first modern roses to have become a generally acknowledged classic. Its pale pink flowers are remontant and beautifully scented. The shape of the flower is pure and beautiful. Very vigorous, quite thorny, it resists disease well and will grow in any position.
Climber: 3 to 5 m (10 to 16 ft). Full sun or partial shade. Diameter of flowers: 8 cm (3 1/4 in), 20–40 petals. Scent***.

Left

Rosa chinensis

'Devoniensis' (× 0.9)

Synonym: 'Magnolia Rose'. Bred by Foster in Great Britain in 1838. Large, creamy-white flowers flushed with yellow and pink are borne continuously on young, mahogany-coloured shoots. Often confused with the climbing form of 'Souvenir de La Malmaison', but even more attractive. For a mild climate (or a micro-climate).
Climber: 2 to 3 m (6 1/2 to 10 ft). Full sun. Diameter of flowers: 9 cm (3 1/2 in), 20–40 petals. Tea scent**.

Facing page

Rosa chinensis

'Bloomfield Abundance' (× 1.90)

Bred by G.C. Thomas in the USA in 1920, this rose has vigorous shoots which put out very long spikes of flowers bearing beautiful little whorled, pale pink roses with long sepals. This very elegant rose flowers from June to the first frosts.
Shrub: 1.5 × 1.2 m (5 × 4 ft) or more. Full sun. Diameter of flowers: 4 cm (1 1/2 in), 20–40 petals. Scent**.

Above

Rosa chinensis

'Cécile Brunner Climbing' (× 0.9)

Bred by Hosp in 1894, this is a mutation of 'Cécile Brunner' and greatly superior in vigour and ease of cultivation. The pale pink flowers are borne continuously from June to the first frosts. Very remontant for a climber.
Climber: 4 m (13 ft) or more. Full sun or partial shade. Diameter of flowers: 4 cm (1 1/2 in), 20–40 petals. Scent**.

Left

Rosa chinensis

'Francis Dubreuil' (× 0.78)

Bred by Dubreuil in 1894. A bush with highly scented, deep crimson flowers, an unusual colour for a Tea Rose. Of moderate vigour, it needs rich soil and a warm position.
Bush: 90 × 60 cm (3 × 2 ft). Full sun and a sheltered position. Diameter of flowers: 7 cm (2 3/4 in), 10–20 petals. Scent***.

Right

Rosa chinensis

'Marie Van Houtte' (× 1.74)

Bred by Ducher in 1871, this rose is the result of a cross between 'Mme de Tartas' and 'Mme Falcot'. It flowers continuously; its blooms varying in colour and shape according to the temperature. They are always very attractive in appearance, shading from ivory to yellow or pale pink.
Bush: 1.3 × 1 m (4 1/4 × 3 1/4 ft). Full sun and a sheltered position. Diameter of flowers: 7 cm (2 3/4 in), 10–20 petals. Tea scent*.

Above

Rosa chinensis

'Mme Laurette Messimy' (× 1.03)

Bred by Guillot in 1887, this is a cross between 'Rival de Paestum' and 'Mme Falcot'. It reliably produces superb flowers of a bright salmon pink. The young shoots are mahogany-coloured. Like all the China Roses, it prefers mild temperatures. Very remontant.
Bush (or shrub when grown in southerly areas): 1.2 × 1 m (4 × 3 1/4 ft). Full sun, sheltered position. Diameter of flowers: 8 cm (3 1/4 in), 10–20 petals. Tea scent*.

Facing page

Rosa chinensis

'Perle d'Or' (× 2.06)

Bred by Dubreuil in 1883, the vigour of this rose varies from one garden to another. It is continuous-flowering, bearing clusters of small, amber-yellow flowers with an orange heart. The petals, of irregular length, curve backwards. Very floriferous.

Bush: 80 × 60 cm (2 3/4 × 2 ft), sometimes more. Full sun. Diameter of flowers: 4 cm (1 1/2 in), 20–40 petals. Tea scent*.

Above

Rosa chinensis

'Viridiflora' (× 0.92)

Synonym: 'The Green Rose'. Discovered in China about 1833. A very remontant rose, with flowers consisting of untidy brown and green bracts. A curiosity. For growing as an exotic feature in the garden or for flower arrangements.
Bush: 1 m × 70 cm (3 1/4 × 2 1/4 ft).

Full sun. Diameter of flowers: 4 cm (1 1/2 in), 10– 20 petals.

Facing page

Rosa × *noisettiana*

'Alister Stella Gray' (× 1.62)

A continuous-flowering Noisette Tea bred by Gray in 1894. Pointed buds open to produce scented flowers with incurving petals, ranging in colour from yellow to white. Slow-growing. Small climber: 2.5 × 1.5 m (8 1/4 × 5 ft). Full sun. Diameter of flowers: 6 cm (2 1/2 in), 20–40 petals. Scent*.

Left

Rosa chinensis sanguinea (× 0.98)

Synonym: 'Bengal Crimson'. A seedling of *Rosa chinensis* 'Semperflorens' discovered in China in 1887. Likes mild temperatures. The colour of its red flowers is outstanding. Continuous-flowering, slow-growing. Shrub: 1.5 × 1.2 m (5 × 4 ft). Full sun. Diameter of flowers: 6 cm (2 1/2 in), 5 petals. Scent*.

Right

Rosa chinensis

'Mutabilis' (× 0.54)

Synonym: *Rosa turkistanica.* Of unknown origin, but in cultivation since 1896, this is one of the most floriferous of all roses. It tolerates hot climates, and has a graceful habit of growth. Its single flowers change from orange-yellow to pink and then deep carmine. They are borne from spring to the first frosts.
Shrub: 1.5 to 2 × 1.5 m (5 to 6 1/2 × 5 ft). Full sun. Diameter of flowers: 6 cm (2 1/2 in), 5 petals. Fruits. Tea scent*.

Below

Rosa × noisettiana

'William Allen Richardson' (× 1)

A Noisette Tea bred by Mme Ducher in 1878, a mutation of 'Rêve d'Or'. Trained against a warm wall it will flower continuously, with orange-yellow blooms from spring to the first frosts. Coppery foliage. Climber: 3 m (10 ft). Full sun. Diameter of flowers: 7 cm (2 ¾ in), 20–40 petals. Scent**.

Right

Rosa × noisettiana

'Mme Alfred Carrière' (× 0.53)

A Noisette Tea bred by J. Schwartz in 1879. Perhaps the most popular of all climbing roses in England. Very floriferous, delicately scented, with pale pink flowers. A rose of very romantic appearance, undemanding and easy to grow: an excellent classic variety which deserves a good situation, neither windy nor too cold.
Climber: 4 m (13 ft) or more. Full sun or partial shade. Diameter of flowers: 8 cm (3 ¼ in), 20–40 petals. Scent*** (in quality rather than intensity).

Left

Rosa × *noisettiana*

'Rêve d'Or' (× 0.86)

A Noisette Tea bred by Mme Ducher in 1869. The easiest to grow of the yellow-flowered Noisette varieties. The young shoots are deep red, the foliage smooth and pale green. The flowers range through warm tones of yellow to pinkish-ochre depending on temperature, and after a few repeat flowerings in summer will produce a fine flush in autumn.
Climber: 4 m (13 ft). Full sun. Diameter of flowers: 8 cm (3 1/4 in), over 40 petals. Tea scent**.

Left

Rosa × borboniana

'Variegata di Bologna' (× 0.78)

Bred by Bonfiglioli in 1909. It is the most strikingly marked of the striped roses. The flowers are cup-shaped, full, and deliciously scented. It may suffer from black spot.
Bush: 1.4 × 1 m (4 1/2 × 3 1/4 ft). Full sun or partial shade. Diameter of flowers: 8 cm (3 1/4 in), over 40 petals. Scent***.

Facing page

Rosa × borboniana

'Souvenir de La Malmaison' (× 2.82)

Synonym: 'Queen of Beauty'. This rose, bred by Beluze in 1843, is among the most beautiful and famous of all old roses. It is remarkable for the size of the corollas, tinged with pink and fading to ivory, and the quartered arrangement of the petals. Flowering is remontant until autumn. Of moderate vigour, it prefers well-drained soil.
Tall bush: 60 cm × 1 m (2 × 3 1/4 ft). Full sun or partial shade. Diameter of flowers: 9 cm (3 1/2 in), over 40 petals. Scent*.

Above

Rosa × borboniana

'Baron J. B. Gonella' (× 0.81)

Bred by Guillot in 1859, this rose is probably a descendant of the very beautiful variety 'Louise Odier', which has equally strong growth. The pink of the large, cup-shaped flowers suggests raspberries, and so does their scent. Excellent for arrangements.
Shrub: 1.6 × 1.2 m (5 1/2 × 4 ft). Full sun. Diameter of flowers: 8 cm (3 in), over 40 petals. Scent***. Remontant.

Right

Rosa × borboniana

'Mme Isaac Pereire' (× 0.25)

Bred by Garçon in 1881, this small climber has strong stems with very large carmine-pink flowers arranged along them. Excellent for clothing a small wall or architectural feature, but not vigorous enough to cover a large surface.
Small climber: 2.5 × 1.5 m (8 1/4 × 5 ft). Full sun or partial shade. Diameter of flowers: 10 cm (4 in), over 40 petals. Scent***.

Above

Rosa × borboniana

'Louise Odier' (× 1.04)

Bred by Margottin in 1851, its vigour makes it one of the best Bourbon Roses. The cupped flowers, as regular in shape as little cabbages, are a clear pink sometimes tinged with lilac, and appear in small clusters from spring until the first frosts. They have a delicious fragrance.
Shrub: its growth varies a great deal from one garden to another, ranging from 1.5 to 3 m (5 to 10 ft). Full sun. Diameter of flowers: 6 cm (2 1/2 in), over 40 petals. Scent***.

Right

Hybrid Perpetual

'Baron Girod de l'Ain' (× 0.48)

Bred by Reverchon in 1897, its white-edged red flowers must have been sensational at the end of the nineteenth century. They are strongly scented. As with many Hybrid Perpetuals, its vigour is not always reliable.
Bush: 1.2 m × 90 cm (4 × 3 ft). Full sun. Diameter of flowers: 8 cm (3 1/4 in), 20–40 petals. Scent***.

Left

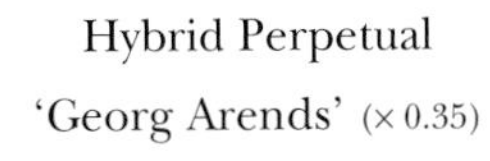

Hybrid Perpetual

'Georg Arends' (× 0.35)

Bred by Hinner in 1910, this rose is one of the most vigorous in its group. Its pale pink flowers are shell-like and prettily shaped. It has few thorns and repeat-flowers well.
Bush: 1.2 m × 90 cm (4 × 3 ft). Full sun. Diameter of flowers: 9 cm ($3\ ^{1}/_{2}$ in), 20–40 petals. Scent**.

Below

Hybrid Perpetual

'Louise Crette' (× 0.89)

Bred by Chambord in 1915. The pure white, perfectly shaped flowers make this an exceptional rose, although it is never grown in gardens today. Healthy, with good repeat-flowering.
Bush: 1 m × 80 cm ($3\ ^{1}/_{4} \times 2\ ^{3}/_{4}$ ft). Full sun. Diameter of flowers: 9 cm ($3\ ^{1}/_{2}$ in), 20– 40 petals. Scent*.

Right

Climbing Hybrid Tea

'Guinée' (× 0.6)

Bred in 1938 by Mallerin, who was aiming to produce the most velvety possible of deep reds, and succeeded. The rose also has a delicious scent. However, it is not particularly vigorous, and does not like hot climates.
Climber: 3 m (10 ft). Full sun or partial shade. Diameter of flowers: 9 cm (3 1/2 in), 20–40 petals. Scent***.

Below

Climbing Hybrid Tea

'Sénégal' (× 0.90)

Bred by Mallerin in 1944. A superb variety, graceful in shape, with a wonderful fruity perfume and the colour of a great wine. It also repeat-flowers well.
Climber: 3 m (10 ft). Full sun. Diameter of flowers: 8 cm (3 1/4 in), 20–40 petals. Scent***.

Facing page

Climbing Hybrid Tea

'Souvenir de Georges Pernet' (× 1.70)

Bred by Pernet Ducher in 1927. A spectacular rose, very vigorous, with extremely double, large pink flowers. The stems are strong and thorny. There is some repeat-flowering.
Climber: 3 m (10 ft). Full sun. Diameter of flowers: 10 to 12 cm (4 to 4 3/4 in), over 40 petals. Scent*.

Above

Rosa × fortuniana (× 0.65)

Brought back from China by Robert Fortune, this rose may be a hybrid of *Rosa banksiae* and *Rosa laevigata.* Its large flowers with incurving petals have a violet scent. The foliage resembles that of *Rosa banksiae,* but the stems have strong thorns. For a mild climate or a micro-climate.
Rambler: up to 10 m (33 ft). Partial shade. Diameter of flowers: 7 cm (2 ³/₄ in), over 40 petals. Scent**. Not remontant.

Right

Rosa banksiae lutescens (× 0.95)

Found in China in 1870. Much rarer than *Rosa banksiae lutea,* which has exactly the same habit of growth, it bears flowers of the same buff yellow in April and May. However, they are single and display beautiful, orange-tinged stamens. Thornless or almost thornless. For a mild climate or a micro-climate.
Rambler: up to 10 m (33 ft). Full sun or partial shade. Diameter of flowers: 3 cm (1 ¹/₄ in), 5 petals. Scent*. Not remontant.

Above

Rosa laevigata (× 1.45)

Synonym: 'Cherokee Rose'. Originally from China, its large flowers with their superb stamens appear in May and June. The leaves consist of three leaflets; the foliage is glossy and lasts for much of the winter.

Rambler: up to 10 m (33 ft). Full sun. Diameter of flowers: 9 cm (3 ½ in), 5 petals. Bristly fruits. Scent**. Not remontant.

Left

Rosa bracteata (× 0.85)

Synonym: 'The Macartney Rose'. Lord Macartney brought this rose back from China at the end of the eighteenth century. It flowers continuously from June to the first frosts. With their strange appearance, its buds, rounded, dark leaflets, greyish stems, and fruits make it a unique and easily recognizable rose. For a mild climate or a micro-climate.
Climber: 4 m (13 ft) or more. Full sun or partial shade. Diameter of flowers: 7 cm (2 ¾ in), 5 petals. Fruits. Scent*.

Right

Rosa bracteata

'Mermaid' (× 0.65)

Bred by Paul in 1917, this is a cross between *Rosa bracteata* and a Hybrid Tea. Good vigour is united with the ability to flower continuously, like its parent, from summer to the first frosts. The flowers are pale yellow. It is very thorny.
Vigorous climber: up to 8 m (26 ft). Full sun, although the base of the plant likes to be in the shade. Diameter of flowers: 10 cm (4 in), 5 petals. Scent not strong but delicious**.

Above

Rosa roxburghii

'Roxburghii' (× 1)

This double form of *Rosa roxburghii* was discovered in China and introduced to Europe in 1824. It is continuous-flowering and has very double deep pink corollas, a startling sight among foliage which consists of many leaflets on stems bristling with thorns, and inclined to have flaking bark. Unusual and magnificently exotic. Shrub: 1.5 × 1 m (5 × 3 $^{1}/_{4}$ ft). Full sun. Diameter of flowers: 9 cm (3 $^{1}/_{2}$ in), over 40 petals. Scent*.

Roses to last a lifetime

Sometimes, glancing into an old garden through its ornamental gateway, we may see roses growing near a deserted house, roses that in spite of total neglect are still surviving long after the former occupants have left. To live so long, these roses must have been well cared for in their early years; they felt at home and became well established. Moreover, they fit into their surroundings because they were not chosen at random. Good planting calls for an understanding of where to plant what, and of what effect you want. It is the outcome of planning a garden to please both ourselves and others. Once the roses have been planted, the gardener must then put his mind to growing them well. Although not everything is under our control, it is up to us to turn a small bush with four branches and five roots into a magnificent specimen. Roses adapt with remarkable ease, but they can also be resolutely individual in their behaviour. Two bushes of the same rose variety will not necessarily turn out the same. They may sometimes look different even when planted in the same place, the kind of thing that makes discussion between amateur rose-growers and professionals so fascinating.

Cultivation

Experience and intuition will help you to decide on the best situation for a particular rose variety. However, anyone can plant roses successfully, without any special knowledge, so long as the characteristics of the variety are taken into account. Roses have two basic needs: light and space. Indoors they will certainly die, and even if they are planted in good soil they will not grow if they are stifled by other plants around them.

Climate

Roses do not like extreme conditions. If the temperature is very high, they will need water, and some like a little shade; in low temperatures they need some shelter. If there is a great deal of rain in your area, they will prefer a well-drained soil. In fact they do not care for anything in excess, but they will still adapt to many different climates.

It is tempting to say that roses should ideally be grown in mild, temperate areas, but the magnificent gardens of Scandinavia and the Alps would quickly disprove that statement. The Botanic Conservatory at Gap in the Hautes-Alpes has a magnificent collection of roses growing at an altitude of 1,000 metres (3,300 ft).

Cold

Some varieties are unsuitable for cold climates (temperatures below -10°C, 14°F). They include *Rosa laevigata, Rosa bracteata* and *Rosa banksiae.* However, the majority of roses which make very long shoots (the ramblers*) will tolerate low temperatures. Other varieties to be avoided in cold areas are the roses bred by the Nabonnand family, who worked on the Côte d'Azur (e.g. 'Sénateur Lafollette' and 'Général Schablikine').

At high altitudes, it is better not to try growing *Rosa chinensis* varieties, whose young shoots are easily scorched by frost, or hybrids of *Rosa noisettiana,* or the less vigorous Hybrid Teas, which may not reach their usual dimensions. The bush and shrub roses of the Caninae, Gallicanae and Cinnamomeae sections are the most frost-hardy. Species which grow naturally in the mountains or in northern countries, such as *Rosa pimpinellifolia, Rosa rugosa, Rosa moyesii, Rosa pendulina,* and their hybrids, are all very hardy. Others require only a microclimate produced by the foliage of a tree or the shelter of a wall or hedge. As an added precaution in such climates, you can give the rose some support in winter or cover its foot with bracken. Once they have survived the testing time of their first few years, few roses die of cold.

Heat

A majority of varieties, for instance the Hybrid Perpetuals, probably suffer more from heat than cold. In great heat a remontant rose may refuse to flower again. Mulching is a useful precaution, and has the added advantage of smothering weeds.

The reaction of roses intolerant of heat is sometimes misunderstood. There is no cause for alarm if they lose their leaves; they are simply protecting themselves. It is more of a nuisance when stems begin turning yellow at the tips and then go black right down to the base. In such cases the rose is suffering sunstroke, and the affected parts must be cut back.

In general, the China Roses (of the Banksiae, Laevigatae, and Bracteatae sections) and the Chinenses section tolerate heat best. However, exceptions to the rule are found from Canada to California and from Scandinavia to southern India.

Soil

The rose is a plant for open ground. The amount and volume of soil it needs for its roots should not be underestimated: it requires a minimum 100 litres (3.5 cu ft) of soil.

Frequency of watering will depend on the soil's ability to retain moisture. Roses can resist drought in a good, deep, clayey soil. If the soil is light and sandy you will need to think

about improving it and installing a watering system. The best material for soil improvement is farm manure containing plenty of straw, and rotted down for at least six months (a year in the case of sheep or horse manure). It should be dug in to a depth of about 30 cm (1 ft); there is no point in digging it in any deeper. Composted leaf-mould is very good on chalky soils. If you use artificial fertilizers take care not to overdo the nitrogen. There are few soils to which roses cannot adapt, although some do exist. In all cases, the soil should be well worked to a good depth before planting. Some stones will do no harm; they will retain warmth and drain off excess water, persuading the roses to put out long, deep roots and thus making them more drought-resistant. In very poor soil, such as chalky marl, the rose will take more time to settle in, but the gardener's patience is often rewarded. Species roses in particular give good results in difficult situations. We have to remember, in all cases, that, while gardening books give information about average dimensions and behaviour, the characteristics of the same variety may change from place to place.

Aspect

It is difficult to say what aspect a rose should have, although they all have a basic need for sun. At midsummer a rose should be enjoying a minimum four hours of sunlight a day, and if that cannot be provided it is better to grow something else. Only the variety 'Albéric Barbier' will flourish on no more than an hour of sunlight a day. Other points to watch out for: do not plant a rose where another has grown recently without replacing the soil entirely to a good depth; avoid water dripping from roof gutters; remove any plants whose foliage might compete with the rose and stifle it. It is interesting to see how far geographical latitude, the nature of the soil, and the aspect can influence the colour and size of the flowers. The season plays a part too: on the same plant, spring flowers are not quite the same colour as autumn blooms, which are often deeper (for instance 'Ghislaine de Féligonde'). Roses growing in northern Europe have more petals than roses growing in the Mediterranean countries.

Supporting structures

It is a good idea to decide what supports to use for a climbing or rambling rose before you plant it, since it is difficult to add the supporting structure once the plant is fully grown. Wood is suitable for medium-sized pergolas; its natural, warm look brings out the colours of the roses well. Chestnut or acacia are good, since they are resistant to rotting.

Iron structures enable you to train a rose in beautiful curved shapes, and they will disappear beneath the foliage quite quickly, lightening the look of the whole thing. They are very durable.

A stone wall makes an ideal support for a climber planted at its foot. You will need to provide horizontal wires fastened to the wall at a distance of 40 cm (16 in) from each other, and at least 5 cm (2 in) away from the wall so that air can circulate behind the foliage. If the wall can be reached from above (for instance in a terraced garden) you can plant any kind of climber with stems flexible enough to tumble over the wall in a cascade, such as 'Paul Transon' or 'Adélaïde d'Orléans'.

A tree makes the most spectacular support of all, and is excellent for ramblers. To give the rose a good chance you should avoid tree species with a tendency to sterilize the soil, such as laurels, mulberries, and walnuts, and plant the rose 60 cm (2 ft) away from the trunk, taking care to fill in the planting hole with good soil from somewhere else. For the first few years all you have to do is guide the rose towards the tree trunk with a support, and then you can leave it to nature. You will not need to trim or prune the rose at all. It will be a sensational sight in spring, followed by a fine show of hips in autumn: a real blessing to the gardener, who then has nothing to do but look up and admire his work.

Harmony of colour

One advantage of old roses is that they make good company for each other. All the soft colours go well together: pastel shades, including cream, yellow, pink, and white. Red roses should be used sparingly, in case they extinguish each other. The most difficult colour to fit into a planting scheme is bright orange (not a common colour for roses). Some of the aggressive quality of orange is lost when the planting scheme also includes white roses, but it is accentuated beside dark red. 'Lady Hillingdon' goes well with the red of 'Sénégal' or 'Guinée'. In general, the pale colours are good at harmonizing a colour scheme.
The question of colours cannot be considered in isolation. The different densities of rose foliage should also be taken into account. If you want to plant a rose hedge, for instance, it is not a good idea to grow *Rosa rugosa*, which has dense foliage, with a China Rose that has a lighter habit of growth and small leaves. Varieties grown on a pergola must of course be of similar vigour, so that none of them ends up overwhelming its neighbour.

Classification of roses by height

You should think about the height to which a variety will grow when you are deciding what will suit a certain position best.

Bush roses

There are not many old roses less than 60 cm (2 ft) tall. The smallest are among the *Rosa chinensis* varieties and the Polyanthas, such as 'Mignonette' and 'Petite Françoise'. They are all very remontant. In fact our idea of a small rose bush derives from the rose-growers of the 1940s to 1960s, who marketed varieties (the

Floribundas) that were specially bred to suit flower-beds in the French style. "Miniature" roses were fashionable at the beginning of the twentieth century and are particularly suited to container growing.

Most of the oldest roses are bushes that grow to a height of 1–1.5 m (3 1/4–5 ft). They include *Rosa gallica* and a considerable number of hybrids such as *Rosa × damascena, Rosa × centifolia, Rosa × centifolia muscosa, Rosa × portlandica,* and *Rosa × borboniana.* They are good in flower-beds, there is an immense range, and they are very easy to grow. Their flowers are all beautiful.

The Hybrid Perpetuals make attractive bushes with their large, remontant, scented flowers, but their sparse foliage, rigid habit of growth, and proneness to disease are disadvantages. However, they can be surrounded with perennials, grasses, and other leafy plants to compensate for these drawbacks.

Shrub roses

Shrubs are roses that will grow to above 1.5 m (5 ft) without a stake to support them. This category includes a large number of species roses, the hybrids of *Rosa alba,* and all bush varieties related to the roses mentioned above once they grow taller than 1.5 m (5 ft).

On the borderline between bushes and shrubs, since their height varies (depending on the soil) between 1.3 and 2 m (4 1/4 and 6 1/2 ft) are the Hybrid Musks bred by Joseph Pemberton and his associates. 'Buff Beauty', 'Félicia', and 'Cornelia' are among these hardy, floriferous, and very disease-resistant roses, which can be planted with confidence. They are repeat-flowering and have a good scent. They do best in rich, fertile soil, where they can become impressive shrubs.

Some shrub roses may reach the dimensions of a small tree: species roses such as *Rosa roxburghii, Rosa henryi, Rosa californica plena, Rosa willmottiae,* and *Rosa moyesii.* A similar effect can be created with certain roses usually regarded as climbers but grown in the open as specimen shrubs. 'Ghislaine de Féligonde', for instance, responds well to being grown in this way. As specimens, they can reach a height of over 3 m (10 ft), and they develop an attractive habit of growth with their arching branches covered with flowers.

Climbers

Climbing roses need support and something against which they can be trained, or at least something to lean on. Wind can do them a great deal of damage if they are not securely tied in.

The hybrids of *Rosa multiflora, Rosa wichuraiana,* and *Rosa luciae* make magnificent climbers to provide romantic shade at key points in the garden, for instance growing over arbours or pergolas. They are all scented, vigorous, and very easy to grow. Most of them flower only once.

Climbing Hybrid Teas have beautiful, attractive flowers; their foliage is not particularly dense and can be prone to disease, and they are only moderately vigorous. Their stems, often hard and thorny, are not nearly as flexible as those of the non-remontant climbers mentioned above. However, their autumn flowering is very attractive, and it makes up for the occasional drawbacks of these varieties, which can sometimes be rather delicate. They are excellent for setting off an architectural feature such as a porch, and are distinguished more for their colours and beautiful scent than for their foliage.

The hybrids of *Rosa noisettiana* range through many soft shades of white and yellow. The flowers, of medium size, have many petals, often undulating ('Rêve d'Or') and sometimes incurving at the centre ('Alister Stella Gray'). Their virtues are remontancy, good scent, and vigour, and a delicate charm partly due to colour differences between the buds and the full-blown flowers. They like warmth, even 'Madame Alfred Carrière', which is often said to like a north aspect.

Ramblers

These roses grow exuberantly. They do not suffer from disease, and are decorative at any season. This group includes *Rosa helenae, Rosa sempervirens, Rosa arvensis, Rosa filipes, Rosa bracteata, Rosa banksiae, Rosa wichuraiana, Rosa setigera, Rosa multiflora,* and their many hybrids.

They will rapidly make their way into the branches of trees, clamber up walls already overgrown with climbing plants, and cover anything suitable so long as there is nothing to stop their upward progress to the bright sky. They bear large clusters of flowers, followed by small hips, and are excellent for planting in large gardens full of trees.

Bare-root planting

In the open: November to March

If you cannot plant a rose as soon as you have bought it, it is best to take some precautions. Heel the plant in, placing it in a small trench filled in with soil, and then water it. Sheltered from the air, the roots will be in no danger of drying out, and planting can be put off to a later date. To be on the safe side, it is best to plant no later than 20 March.

Plant roses in well-worked soil. Dig a hole measuring 40 cm (16 in) in all directions, and put your rose into it. Planting is a solemn moment, with the promise of magical results.

The roots can be refreshed by simply cutting them back; there is no need to make a sloping cut. Leave the label in place if the plant has one; you will not regret doing so, particularly as it will soon disappear among the foliage. (If there are any problems later, a professional will find it difficult to advise you if you cannot identify the variety.) Place a mixture of soil and well-rotted manure at the bottom of the hole. Holding the plant with one hand to ensure that the union* is just level with the surface of the soil, arrange the roots in their natural position and fill the hole in with fine, crumbly soil. Firm it all around the plant with the flat of your hands, and water even if the soil is moist, to get rid of any air. In cold areas it may be a good idea to earth up the plant, but only until winter is over.

Container planting

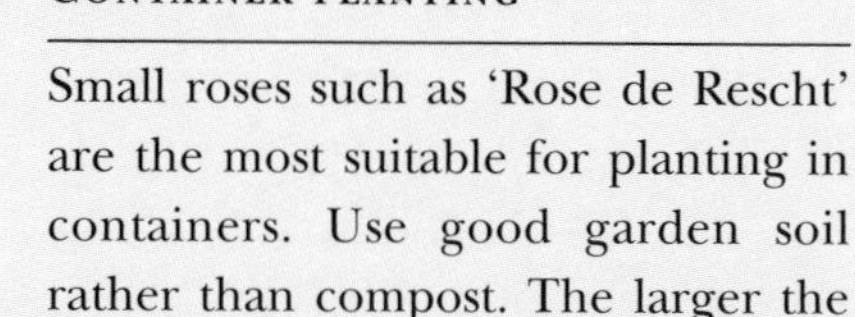

Small roses such as 'Rose de Rescht' are the most suitable for planting in containers. Use good garden soil rather than compost. The larger the container (its volume must be over 50 litres, 1.75 cu ft) the better the rose will grow; roses hate to be short of space, and a climber grown in a pot would very soon run out of soil.

Care of roses

In general, roses are not demanding, but they do need a minimum of care. Among their dislikes are: being invaded by weeds, not enough soil around the neck* of the plant to keep it from moving in the planting hole so that it suffers from wind-rock, injury to the stems, and having to spend all summer without a drop of water.

Their likes include: manure when they are planted, regular hoeing to keep weeds down, watering and mulching in summer, and the removal of all weak or dead wood and diseased foliage.

Since roses regenerate very easily, it is best to keep only young, healthy wood on the plant as far as possible. Strong suckers* may appear, coming up from the root system. They can be recognized by the difference of their foliage and if they are from a rose grafted on a rootstock* they should be removed at once. Place a foot against the stock to hold it steady and pull away the sucker from the base.

Fungal diseases

Mildew can appear on some susceptible varieties as soon as the weather turns warm. First a white down-like or powdery substance appears on the buds and the stems, then the leaves crumple up. Dust the foliage and foot of the plant with sulphur at the end of April, and repeat the treatment in early July. As a precaution, it is a good idea to treat all susceptible varieties every year. This disease sometimes affects roses trained on a warm wall which reflects back too much heat. You should move the roses to partial shade, or move the supporting structures further away from the wall to allow more air to circulate.

Symptomatic of Marsonia rosae, or black spot, is the appearance on the leaves of yellow spots, which then turn black. The leaves will fall prematurely. Black spot affects some roses more than others. Even after trying the best synthetic fungicides, we would still recommend winter treatment with Bordeaux mixture as a preventive measure. The best method, however, is to cut away all diseased parts (remove them entirely, and do not leave them on the ground). The rose will then begin growing on young, healthy wood again. If black spot persists, you could try moving the plant during the next winter after cutting it back hard, and planting it in a different aspect, in better-drained soil.

Pests

The appearance of ladybirds, those useful predators, is a sign of the presence of the aphids on which they prey; the ladybirds have a great deal of work to do, and you should not interrupt it by using an unsuitable insecticide. Aphids attack roses when the plants are full of sap; you can help to prevent such an attack by not feeding your roses with fertilizer at this time. The aphid colony will go away when the flowers come out, since there is less sap in the plant by then.

If you have a severe infestation, you can spray the plant in the evening with a rotenone-based insecticide.

Pruning

It is best not to prune in freezing weather or when it is raining. Use clean, sharp secateurs and prune more lightly as the plant grows older. To achieve good proportions, you should take a good look at the plant before you start pruning, first from a distance and then at close quarters.

– Pruning remontant roses: *end of winter*

Bushes

Decide which stems are worth keeping (the youngest and most attractive) and cut all the others right back to the base. Shorten the selected stems by one-third, making a sloping cut above and opposite an outward-facing bud.

Shrubs and climbers

Prune in the same way; you may need a pruning saw for large stems.

– Pruning non-remontant roses: *after flowering, or at the end of winter for roses with decorative fruits*

Bushes, shrubs, climbers

After flowering these roses will make a large quantity of new growth which will carry the best flowers next season, so they should not be removed. However, old, distorted, weak, or very dark stems should be taken out at the base during the summer. You will often need to go over the plant again in spring to improve its shape and shorten the young wood slightly. Hips are borne on the old wood, and if they are attractive you will not want to cut it back until the end of winter. However, pruning is often unnecessary and can be confined to removing any unattractive parts of the plant.

– Pruning for hygiene: *all the year round*

When you are removing diseased parts of a plant, you should disinfect your tools first with alcohol or diluted disinfectant. Dead-heading the faded blooms between flowerings will encourage the plants to produce more blooms and make the garden look more attractive.

Propagation

Roses can be propagated by various methods: from seeds and cuttings, by layering, by division, and by budding or grafting.

Seedlings

Seeds will not produce plants true to the variety, but seedlings are used to provide rootstocks (of wild roses) and in the breeding of new varieties. You may discover worthwhile self-sown seedlings in your garden.

Cuttings

If you want to ensure the survival of a certain variety you can try taking a cutting at any time of year. All you have to do is put a 15 cm (6 in) section of stem in the ground in partial shade, and water it in. You will have to wait a year before you move the rooted cutting to its permanent position. Success rates differ according to the variety. Some roses grow easily from cuttings, while others never will.

Layering

Layering consists of rooting a low-growing branch by forcing part of it down into the ground. The layered section is not separated from the mother plant for several months, by which time it has formed its own roots and can grow on them.

Division

A variety growing on its own roots can also be propagated (when the soil is moist) by detaching one of the suckers and planting it. Or if a rose develops an adventitious* shoot it can be removed, giving you a stem with a brown area, part stem and part root, with rootlets.* Cut back the upper part of the stem and plant carefully.

Budding (shield grafting)

This is the method used by professionals. It is done in summer on rootstocks prepared to receive the scion,* a bud detached from the variety you want to propagate. The scion is introduced under the bark of the stock in a slit made at the point of union. The budding operation is also termed "shield grafting". Once the scion is inserted, the union is bandaged with a latex tie or raffia. The following year the bud will begin to grow once the stems of the stock above it have been removed. The result is a plant with the hardy roots of a wild rose, while the upper parts are those of the budded variety. This technique is very widely used and gives good results, but there is always a percentage of failures. Nature can never be entirely tamed.

Preserving old roses

The varieties most widely grown are much in demand from rose nurseries because they have proved their worth. On the other hand, we tend to copy what we have admired elsewhere, so the same roses are found in gardens again and again. It can, however, be fascinating to grow varieties now on their way to extinction – so many wonderful roses are hardly grown at all. They do feature in rose collections or "conservatory" rose gardens, but they are represented by only a small number of plants, so that their survival is at risk. And looking at such collections, it is hard to imagine these roses blooming in the wild.

It is well worth trying to preserve an old, neglected rose that has taken root among stones, or is growing among ruins or on waste land, threatened by modern air pollution. Suppose you have moved into a new house and find some old roses, apparently in a bad way: it is worth cutting them back hard and then leaving them for at least a year or so to see what you have, before you give up on them.

A gardener who combines curiosity with a wish to preserve unusual roses can also venture on planting rare varieties for both their experimental and their decorative value. As we give new life to these Sleeping Beauties, they will have many a tale to tell us.

Glossary

Adventitious: occurring sporadically or not in the usual location.
Bract: a modified leaf with an inflorescence growing in its axil.
Breeder: the person who breeds a new variety by artificial fertilization and can claim to be publicly acknowledged as its creator. Today, newly bred varieties have to be certified.
Bud: the bud growing in the axil between leaf and stem, which will develop into a new shoot.
Clone: from Greek *klōn*, twig or slip. All the plants produced from the same plant propagated by vegetative means (non-sexual). All individual members of a clone are thus genetically identical. Budding is a means of obtaining a clone.
Corolla: the combination of the petals of a flower.
Floriferous: producing a great many flowers.
Hybrid: the result of a cross between two different species, or between a species and a variety, or between two varieties.
Incurved: term used to describe the central petals of a flower when they remain folded in on themselves instead of opening out.
Introduction: term for the first occurrence of the growing of a plant in a country where it is not native, in order to acclimatize and propagate it.
Leaflet: each of the divisions of a compound leaf is called a leaflet.
Neck: the transition area between the roots and stems of roses. The union of grafted roses is at the neck.
Rambler: a climbing rose of very vigorous growth, with long, supple stems from the base, able to reach a great height and cover trees, buildings, etc.
Remontant: also "repeat-flowering", said of a rose which flowers again at least once after the first, early summer flush of blooms.
Rootlets: fine, numerous ramifications running from the main roots.
Rootstock: name given to the wild rose roots and base of stem on which grafting or budding of a cultivated variety is performed.
Scion: the bud of the rose variety grafted on a wild rootstock.
Sections: subdivisions of the genus Rosa into which species showing similar characteristics and obviously related are grouped.
Species: the criteria by which a species is identified are that its individual members obviously resemble each other, and they will breed.
Stamen: male organ of reproduction, consisting of a filament and an anther, with two loculi from which the pollen emerges.
Stigma (pl. stigmata): upper, sticky part of the pistil (the female organ of the flower) on which the pollen is deposited to fertilize it.
Stipule: small leaf-like excrescences at the base of the leaf stem. When present, there are two stipules to the leaf stem.
Style: from Greek, *stulos* (column). The area of the pistil (the female organ) ending in the stigmata, where the pollen is deposited. In roses they are sometimes separate and sometimes fused.
Sucker: a shoot growing from underground rather than the main stem of the plant, put out from a root. If a rose is growing on its own roots, such a shoot can be used to propagate it by division; if it is a grafted rose the sucker will belong to the rootstock and will deprive the grafted variety of strength, so it should be removed.
Type: the most representative wild member of a species.
Union: the point at which the bud of a variety is grafted on the wild rootstock.
Variety: from Latin *variare*, to vary. Subdivision of a species containing individuals all presenting special characteristics genetically transmitted. Varieties are usually the result of breeding.

Bibliography

Modern works

BEALES PETER, *Classic Roses*, Collins Harvill, 1985.

BEUCHER PATRICIA, *Roses anciennes*, Nathan, 1993.

BOULLARD BERNARD, *Dictionnaire de botanique*, Ellipses, 1988.

HARKNESS JACK, *The Makers of Heavenly Roses*, Souvenir Press, 1985.

HAUDEBOURG MARIE-THÉRÈSE, *Roses et jardins*, Hachette, 1995.

JACOB ANNY, GRIMM HEIDI and WERNT, MULLER BRUNO, and HUMERY JACQUELINE, *Rose anciennes et roses sauvages*, Eugen Ulmer, 1992.

PHILLIPS ROGER and RIX MARTYN, *The Quest for the Rose*, BBC Books, 1993.

TESTU CHARLOTTE, *Les Roses anciennes*, La Maison Rustique, 1984.

THOMAS GRAHAM STUART, *The Graham Stuart Thomas Rose Book*, John Murray, 1994.

Older works

BELMONT ABEL, *Dictionnaire de la rose*, E. Drosne, 1896.

COCHET-COCHET AND MOTTET S., *Les Rosiers*, Octave Doin et Librairie Agricole, 1897.

FORTUNE ROBERT, *A Journey to the Tea Countries of China and India*, John Murray, 1853.

GRAVEREAUX JULES, *Les Roses cultivées à L'Haÿ en 1902*, 1902.

PEMBERTON R. P. JOSEPH H., *Roses*, Longmans, Green and Co., 1908.

Index

Page numbers refer to text or captions, except those in italic, which indicate illustrations.

'Adélaide d'Orléans', *87*, 114
'Alain Blanchard', *55*
'Albéric Barbier', 114
'Albertine', 9
'Alexandre Girault', *77*
'Alfred de Dalmas', *41*
'Alister Stella Gray', *98*, 117
'Apothecary's Rose', 11, 12, 14
'Assemblage des Beautés', 9, *55*
'Baron Girod de l'Ain', *104*
'Baron J.B. Gonella', *103*
'Belle de Crécy', 7, *57*
'Belle Isis', *57*
'Bengal Crimson', *98*
'Béranger', *41*
'Betty Sherriff', *74*
'Bizarre Triomphant', *60, 61*
'Black Moss', 42
'Bloomfield Abundance', *93*
'Blush Damask', *46*
'Buff Beauty', 116
'Camaïeux', *58*
'Canary Bird', 20
'Cardinal de Richelieu', *59*
'Cécile Brunner', 93
'Cécile Brunner' Climbing, *93*
'Celestial', 7
'Chapeau de Napoléon', 34
'Charles de Mills', *60, 61*
'Cherokee Rose', *109*
'Chevette Rose', 11
Climbing Hybrid Tea 'Guinée', *106*
Climbing Hybrid Tea 'Sénégal', *106*
Climbing Hybrid Tea 'Souvenir de Georges Pernet', *106*
'Complicata', *63*
'Comte de Chambord', *71*
'Cornelia', *75*, 116
'Crimson Rambler', *81*, 88
'Cristata', *34*
'Cuisse de Nymphe', 7, *16*, 19
'Dart's Defender', *24*
'Devoniensis', *91*
'Duchesse de Montebello', *64*
'Duchesse de Rohan', *46*
'Éléonore Berkeley', *82*
'Étoile de Hollande', 10
'Eugénie Guinoisseau', *42*
'Evangéline', *88*
'Fairy, The', 9
'Fantin-Latour', *36*
'Félicia', 116
'Félicité Parmentier', *19*
'Four Seasons Rose of Paestum, The', *53*
'Francis Dubreuil', *94*
'François Juranville', *78*, 79
'Frau Dagmar Hastrup', *31*
'Général Schablikine', 10, 113
'Georg Arends', *105*
'Ghislaine de Féligonde', *82*, 114, 116
'Green Rose, The', 97
'Grüss an Aachen', 6
'Guinée', *106*, 115
'Hansa', 24
'Henri Martin', *42*
Hildesheim Rose, The, 11
'Hippolyte', *63*
Hybrid Musk 'Cornelia', *75*
Hybrid Musk 'Felicia', 116
Hybrid Musk 'Nur Mahal', *76*
Hybrid Musk 'Queen of the Musks', *77*
Hybrid Perpetual 'Baron Girod de l'Ain', *104*
Hybrid Perpetual 'Georg Arends', *105*
Hybrid Perpetual 'Louise Crette', *105*
Hybrid Teas, 6, 9, 10, 113
'Ispahan', *48*
'Jacques Cartier', 9, *71*
'Jenny Duval', *64*
'Juno', *36*
'Kathleen Harrop', 9
'Königin von Dänemark', *19*
'La Belle Sultane', 68
'La Royale', 7
'La Séduisante', 7
'La Ville de Bruxelles', *48*
'La Virginale', 7
'Labrador Rose, The', 8
'Lady Hillingdon', 115
'Laure Davoust', *85*
'Léontine Gervais', *79*
'Louis Van Till', *64*
'Louise Crette', *105*
'Louise Odier', 103
'Macartney Rose, The', *110*
'Mme Alfred Carrière', *100*, 117
'Mme de Tartas', 94
'Mme Falcot', 94, 95
'Mme Isaac Pereire', *103*
'Mme Laurette Messimy', 78, *95*
'Mme Louis Lévêque', *12*
'Magnolia Rose', 91
'Maheka', 68
'Maiden's Blush', 7, 16
'Marbrée', *72*
'Marie Van Houtte', *94*
'Mermaid', 10, *110*
'Mignonette', 9, *86*, 115
'Mousseline', 41
'Mousseuse Blanche', 39
'Mutabilis', *98*
'Naissance de Vénus', *19*
'New Dawn', *90*
'New Maiden's Blush', *19*
'Nuits de Young', *42*
'Nur Mahal', *76*
'Officinalis', 11, 12, 14
'Old Blush', 9
'Old Velvet Rose', *44*
'Omar Khayyam', *51*
'Orpheline de Juillet', *66*
'Paquerette', 86
'Parks' Yellow Tea-Scented China', 12
'Parson's Pink China', 9
'Paul Transon', *79*, 114
'Perle d'Or', *97*
'Perpétuelle Mousseuse', 51
'Petite Françoise', 115
'Petite Lisette', *38*
Polyantha Rose 'Grüss an Aachen', *6*
Polyantha Rose 'Mignonette', *86*
'Princesse Louise', *88*
'Provins Rose, The', 14
'Quatre Saisons Blanc Mousseux', *51*
'Queen of Beauty', *103*
'Queen of the Musks', *77*
'Rayon d'Or', 13
'Red Moss', 42
'Reine du Danemark', *19*
'Rêve d'Or', 9, 100, 101, 117
'Rhodophile Gravereaux', 22
'Rival de Paestum', 95
Rosa acicularis, 7
Rosa arvensis, 9, 117
Rosa banksiae, 10, 108, 113, 117
Rosa banksiae lutea, 10, 108
Rosa banksiae lutescens, *108*
Rosa blanda, 8
Rosa bracteata, 10, *110*, 113, 117
Rosa bracteata 'Mermaid', *110*
Rosa brunonii, 9
Rosa californica plena, 116
Rosa canina, 8, 14, 16
Rosa carnea, 7
Rosa carolina, 8
Rosa centifolia major, 34
Rosa chinensis, 9, 13, 86, 113
Rosa chinensis 'Bloomfield Abundance', *93*
Rosa chinensis 'Cécile Brunner Climbing', *93*
Rosa chinensis 'Devoniensis', *91*
Rosa chinensis 'Francis Dubreuil', *94*
Rosa chinensis 'Général Schablikine', *10*
Rosa chinensis 'Mme Laurette Messimy', 78, *95*
Rosa chinensis 'Marie Van Houtte', *94*
Rosa chinensis 'Mutabilis', *98*
Rosa chinensis 'Perle d'Or', *97*
Rosa chinensis 'Semperflorens', 98
Rosa chinensis 'Viridiflora', *97*
Rosa damascena, 10, 12, 15, 19
Rosa damascena 'Kazanlik', 15
Rosa damascena perpetual, *53*
Rosa farreri, 8
Rosa farreri persetosa, *25*
Rosa fedtschenkoana, 8, 12, *28*
Rosa filipes, 117
Rosa foetida, 8, 13, 22
Rosa foliolosa, 8
Rosa gallica, 9, 10, 15, *34*, 63, 71, 116
Rosa gallica 'Alain Blanchard', *55*
Rosa gallica 'Assemblage des Beautés', 9, *55*
Rosa gallica 'Belle de Crécy', *57*
Rosa gallica 'Belle Isis', *57*
Rosa gallica 'Camaïeux', *58*
Rosa gallica 'Cardinal de Richelieu', *59*
Rosa gallica 'Charles de Mills', *60, 61*

Rosa gallica 'Complicata', *63*
Rosa gallica 'Duchesse de Montebello', *64*
Rosa gallica 'Jenny Duval', *64*
Rosa gallica 'Louis Van Till', *64*
Rosa gallica 'Maheka', *68*
Rosa gallica 'Orpheline de Juillet', *66*
Rosa gallica 'Tuscany', *67*
Rosa gallica versicolor, 68
Rosa gallica 'Ville de Londres', *68*
Rosa gallica 'Violacea', *68*
Rosa gigantea, 9
Rosa helenae, 9, *74,* 117
Rosa henryi, 116
Rosa hugonis, 7, 8
Rosa kordesii, 13
Rosa laevigata, 10, 108, *109,* 113
Rosa luciae, 9, 78, 117
Rosa luciae 'Alexandre Girault', *77*
Rosa luciae 'François Juranville', *78*
Rosa luciae 'Léontine Gervais', *79*
Rosa luciae 'Paul Transon', *79*
Rosa macrantha, 63, 71
Rosa macrantha 'Waitziana', *71*
Rosa moschata, 9
Rosa moyesii, 8, *26,* 113, 116
Rosa mulliganii, 16, 74
Rosa multibracteata, 8, *15*
Rosa multiflora, 9, 12, 81, 86, 117
Rosa multiflora 'Crimson Rambler', *81*
Rosa multiflora 'Éléonore Berkeley', *82*
Rosa multiflora 'Ghislaine de Féligonde', *82*
Rosa multiflora inermis, 81
Rosa multiflora 'Laure Davoust', *85*
Rosa multiflora 'Veilchenblau', *85*
Rosa multiflora 'Violette', *86*
'Rosa Mundi', *68*
Rosa nitida, 8, 24
Rosa nitida 'Dart's Defender', *24*
Rosa noisettiana, 113, 117
Rosa omeiensis, 8
Rosa omeiensis chrysocarpa, 20
Rosa palustris, 8
Rosa pendulina, 8, 113
Rosa pernettiana 'Rhodophile Gravereaux', *22*
Rosa pimpinellifolia, 8, *22,* 113
Rosa pimpinellifolia 'Single Cherry', *23*
Rosa pomifera, 8
Rosa roxburghii, 11, 29, 111, 116
Rosa roxburghii 'Normalis', 11
Rosa roxburghii 'Rosburghii', 11, *111*
Rosa rubicans, 7
Rosa rubiginosa, 8, *16*
Rosa rubrifolia, 8, *8, 16*
Rosa rubrifolia 'Sir Cedric Morris', *16*
Rosa rugosa, 8, 12, 29, 113, 115
Rosa rugosa 'Frau Dagmar Hastrup', *31*
Rosa rugosa 'Hansa', 24
Rosa rugosa 'Roseraie de l'Haÿ', *31*
Rosa rugosa 'Scabrosa', *33*
Rosa rugosa 'Villa des Tybilles', *33*
Rosa sempervirens, 9, 117
Rosa sempervirens 'Adélaïde d'Orléans', *87*
Rosa sempervirens 'Princesse Louise', *88*
Rosa setigera, 117
Rosa setipoda, 8
Rosa souliena, 12
Rosa sp. 'Betty Sherriff', *74*
Rosa turkistanica, 98
Rosa virginiana, 8
Rosa wichuraiana, 9, 81, 88, 117
Rosa willmottiae, 8, 116
Rosa × *alba,* 8
Rosa × *alba* 'Celestial', 7
Rosa × *alba* 'Cuisse de Nymphe', *16*
Rosa × *alba* 'Félicité Parmentier', *19*
Rosa × *alba* 'Reine du Danemark', *19*
Rosa × *borboniana,* 10, 116
Rosa × *borboniana* 'Baron J.B. Gonella', *103*
Rosa × *borboniana* 'Louise Odier', *104*
Rosa × *borboniana* 'Mme Isaac Pereire', *103*
Rosa × *borboniana* 'Souvenir de La Malmaison', *103*
Rosa × *borboniana* 'Variegata di Bologna', *103*
Rosa × *centifolia,* 9, 10, 13, 15, 116
Rosa × *centifolia* 'Cristata', *34*
Rosa × *centifolia* 'Fantin-Latour', *36*
Rosa × *centifolia* 'Juno', *36*
Rosa × *centifolia* 'Petite Lisette', *38*
Rosa × *centifolia major,* 14, 34, *38*
Rosa × *centifolia muscosa,* 9, 39, 116
Rosa × *centifolia muscosa alba, 39*
Rosa × *centifolia muscosa* 'Alfred de Dalmas', *41*
Rosa × *centifolia muscosa* 'Béranger', *41*
Rosa × *centifolia muscosa* 'Eugénie Guinoisseau', *42*
Rosa × *centifolia muscosa* 'Henri Martin', *42*
Rosa × *centifolia muscosa* 'Mme Louis Lévêque', *12*
Rosa × *centifolia muscosa* 'Nuits de Young', *42*
Rosa × *centifolia muscosa* 'Salet', *44*
Rosa × *centifolia muscosa* 'William Lobb', *44*
Rosa × *damascena,* 9, 116
Rosa × *damascena* 'Blush Damask', *46*
Rosa × *damascena* 'Duchesse de Rohan', *46*
Rosa × *damascena* 'Ispahan', *48*
Rosa × *damascena* 'La Ville de Bruxelles', *48*
Rosa × *damascena* 'Omar Khayyam', *51*
Rosa × *damascena perpetual, 53*
Rosa × *damascena* 'Quatre Saisons Blanc Mousseux', *51*
Rosa × *damascena* 'Rose de Rescht', *53*
Rosa × *damascena* 'Rose des Quatre Saisons', *53*
Rosa × *fortuniana, 108*
Rosa × *micrugosa* 'Walter Butt', *29*
Rosa × *noisettiana,* 9
Rosa × *noisettiana* 'Alister Stella Gray', *98*
Rosa × *noisettiana* 'Mme Alfred Carrière', *100*
Rosa × *noisettiana* 'Rêve d'Or', *100, 101*
Rosa × *noisettiana* 'William Allen Richardson', *100*
Rosa × *odorata,* 9
Rosa × *odorata ochroleuca,* 9, 12
Rosa × *portlandica,* 9, 116
Rosa × *portlandica* 'Comte de Chambord', *71*
Rosa × *portlandica* 'Jacques Cartier', *71*
Rosa × *portlandica* 'Marbrée', *72*
Rosa × *portlandica* 'Yolande d'Aragon', *72*
Rosa × *wichuraiana* 'Evangéline', *88*
Rosa × *wichuraiana* 'New Dawn', *90*
Rosa xanthina, 8, *20*
'Rose de Mai', 15
'Rose des Peintres', 38
'Rose des Quatre Saisons', 9, 12, *53*
'Rose de Rescht', 14, 15, *53,* 118
'Roseraie de l'Haÿ', *31*
'Rosier Blanc Royal', 7
'Rosier de Thionville', 51
'Rosier Rouillé', 16
'Rouge Eblouissante', 55
'Roxburghii', 11, *111*
'Salet', *44*
'Scabrosa', *33*
'Semperflorens', 98
'Sénateur Lafollette', 113
'Sénégal', 106, 115
'Shailer's White Moss', 39
'Single Cherry', *23*
'Sir Cedric Morris', *16*
'Souvenir de Georges Pernet', *106*
'Souvenir de La Malmaison', 91, *103*
'Sweet Briar', 16
'Tuscany', *67*
'Variegata di Bologna', *103*
'Veilchenblau', 9, *85,* 86
'Villa de Tybilles', *33*
'Ville de Londres', *68*
'Violacea', *68*
'Violette', *86*
'Viridiflora', *97*
'Waitziana', *71*
'Walter Butt', *29*
'William Allen Richardson', *100*
'William Lobb', *44*
'Yolande d'Aragon', *72*
'Zéphirine Drouhin', 9

Rose gardens and old rose collections to visit

UNITED KINGDOM
David Austin Roses (plant centre and rose gardens),
Bowling Green Lane, Albrighton, Wolverhampton WV7 3HB

Peter Beales Roses, London Road, Attleborough, Norfolk NR17 1AY and at:
Mannington Gardens, Mannington Hall, Saxthorpe, Norwich NR11 7BB

Cambridge University Botanic Garden, Bateman Street, Cambridge

Gardens of the Rose (Royal National Rose Society), Chiswell Green, St Albans, Herts AL2 3NR

Gardens of the Royal Horticultural Society, Wisley Gardens, Ripley, Surrey

Mottisfont Abbey Rose Garden, Hampshire

Queen Mary Rose Gardens, Regent's Park, London

FRANCE
Roseraie du Val-de-Marne, 8 rue Albert Watel, 94240 L'Haÿ-les-Roses

Conservatoire botanique de Charance, 05000 Gap

Roseraie de Saverne, 66704 Saverne

Roseraie municipale de Quévert, Courtil des Senteurs, 22100 Dinan

Roseraie Saint-Nicolas, 71170 Châlon-sur-Saône

Jardin botanique du Parc de la Tête d'Or, place Leclerc, 69006 Lyon

DENMARK
Rosenplanteskolen I Love, Plantevej 3, 4270 Hong. (Large old rose and garden rose nursery.)

GERMANY
Rosarium Sangerhausen, Steinberger Weg 3, 4700 Sangerhausen. (Large publicly owned collection of old roses.)

ITALY
Large private collection of Professor Fineschi, Cavriglia, San Giovanni Valdarno, Tuscany.

USA
Heirloom Old Garden Roses, 24062 NE Riverside Drive, St Paul, Oregon 97137
Heritage Rose Gardens, Tanglewood Farms, 16831 Mitchel Creek Drive, Fort Bragg, California 95437
Jackson & Perkins, Bear Creek Gardens, PO Box 9100, 2518 S Pacific Highway, Medford, Oregon 97501

Specialist rose nurseries

UNITED KINGDOM
David Austin Roses, Bowling Green Lane, Albrighton, Wolverhampton WV7 3HB

Peter Beales Roses, London Road, Attleborough, Norfolk NR17 1AY

R. Harkness & Co. Ltd, The Rose Gardens, Cambridge Road, Hitchin, Herts SG4 0JT

FRANCE
André Eve (roses anciennes), 45300 Pithiviers-le-Viel.
Roseraie de Berty, 07110 Largentière. Éléonore Cruse, Christian Biette.
Nursery and old rose garden where all the photographs in this book were taken.

Associations

The Royal National Rose Society, Chiswell Green, St Albans, Herts AL2 3NR

Les Amis de la Roseraie du Val-de-Marne, rue Albert Watel, 94240 L'Haÿ-les-Roses, France

Verein Deutscher Rosenfreunde (VDR), Waldseestrasse 14, 7570 Baden-Baden, Germany

Contents

THE ROSE, QUEEN OF FLOWERS 5

The classification of old roses 7
Wild roses 7
The earliest varieties: an enigma 7
Identified varieties 7

The different sections of species and their hybrids 7
The Caninae 8
The Pimpinellifoliae (or burnet roses) 8
The Carolinae 8
The Cinnamomeae 8
The Gallicanae 9
The Synstylae 9
The Chinenses 9

Some sections native to China 10
The Banksiae 10
The Laevigatae 10
The Bracteatae 10
The subgenus Platyrhodon 11

The history of rose-growing 11
Travelling botanists 12
Rose-growing families and their roses 12

The rose, mankind's companion 13
Symbolism and poetry 13

Everyday pleasures 14
Bouquets and flower arrangements 14
Pot-pourri 14
Roses in the kitchen 14
The rose in perfumery 15

The History of the Republic of Roses 15

Illustrations 16

Practical guide:
ROSES TO LAST A LIFETIME 112
Cultivation 113
Climate 113
Cold 113
Heat 113
Soil 113
Aspect 114
Supporting structures 114
Harmony of colour 115

Classification of roses by height 115
Bush roses 115
Shrub roses 116
Climbers 117
Ramblers 117

Bare-root planting 118
In the open: November to March 118
Container planting 118

Care of roses 119
Fungal diseases 119
Pests 119

Pruning 120
Pruning remontant roses 120
Bushes 120
Shrubs and climbers 120
Pruning non-remontant roses 120
Bushes, shrubs, climbers 120
Pruning for hygiene 120

Propagation 120
Seedlings 120
Cuttings 120
Layering 120
Division 121
Budding (shield grafting) 121

Preserving old roses 121

Glossary 122
Bibliography 123
Index 124
Useful addresses 126

EVERGREEN is an imprint of Benedikt Taschen Verlag GmbH

Under the direction of Paul Starosta
Editor: Philippe Pierrelée
Text: Eléonore Cruse
Photographs: Paul Starosta
Cover: Angelika Taschen, Cologne
Translated by Anthea Bell
In association with First Edition Translations Ltd, Cambridge
Realization of the English edition by First Edition Translations Ltd, Cambridge

Printed in Italy
ISBN 3-8228-7761-1